TEDBooks

The Misfit's Manifesto

LIDIA YUKNAVITCH

Artwork by Alex Brewer (HENSE)

TED Books
Simon & Schuster
London New York Toronto Sydney New Delhi

TEDBooks

First published in Great Britain by Simon & Schuster UK Ltd, 2017
A CBS COMPANY

First TED Books hardback edition October 2017

TED, the TED logo and TED Books are trademarks of TED Conference, LLC.
TED BOOKS and colophon are registered trademarks of TED Conferences, LLC.

For more information on licensing the TED talk that accompanies this book,
or other content partnerships with TED, please contact TEDBooks@TED.com.

10 9 8 7 6 5 4 3 2 1

Simon & Schuster UK Ltd
1st Floor
222 Gray's Inn Road
London WC1X 8HB

www.simonandschuster.co.uk
www.simonandschuster.com.au
www.simonandschuster.co.in

Simon & Schuster Australia, Sydney
Simon & Schuster India, New Delhi

The author and publishers have made all reasonable efforts to contact
copyright-holders for permission, and apologise for any omissions or errors
in the form of credits given. Corrections may be made to future printings.

"Untitled" (I shop therefore I am)
Copyright: Barbara Kruger
Courtesy: Mary Boone Gallery, New York

A CIP catalogue record for this book
is available from the British Library

Hardback ISBN: 978-1-4711-6232-9
eBook ISBN: 978-1-4711-6233-6

Interior design by: MGMT.design
Jacket design by: MGMT.design
Jacket art by: Alex Brewer (HENSE)

Printed and bound by CPI Group (UK) Ltd, Croydon, CR0 4YY

MIX
Paper from
responsible sources
FSC   FSC® C020471
www.fsc.org

Simon & Schuster UK are committed to sourcing paper that is made
from wood grown in sustainable forests and support the Forest Stewardship
Council, the leading international forest certification organisation. Our
books displaying the FSC logo are printed on FSC certified paper.

If anyone has ever made you feel like you were nothing, then this book is for you

CONTENTS

The Misfit's Manifesto

Misfit.

Trust me when I say there is a lot packed into that little word.

First let me tell you what it doesn't mean. I'm not talking about how we all, on occasion, feel weird, or lonely, or exhausted, or like a failure, or left out. Everyone feels those things sometimes. That's the human default. I'm not talking about feeling out of place or awkward. I'm not talking about chafing against social roles, or losing one's way, or midlife crises, though all those states of being are important and worth honoring.

There are so very many ways to define the word *misfit*. Most of the definitions "out there" involve some version of the following: a person who is different from other people and who does not seem to belong in a particular group or situation, or someone or something that fits badly, or a person who is poorly adapted to a new situation or environment.

The first definition for *misfit* on *Urban Dictionary* goes like this:

Basically, an individual. In the school social classes of today, a misfit doesn't fit into any one clique quite right, not even the outcasts, but may have qualities of each one. True misfits usually do not believe they fit categories like emo or goth, and they are often introverts. Misfits tend to follow their own beliefs, and are usually persecuted for it. Misfits tend to be outcast for no reason, have few good friends, and are usually intelligent and mature, and sometimes sort of insane and depressed, and nearly always creative beyond measure. Misfits tend not to care about their bad social lives, but some do.

That quiet, depressed girl over there is a misfit[1].

Others might say that the artist with the blue hair in the corner is a misfit.

That computer nerd building his own time machine in his basement is a misfit.

That guy wearing the anarchist jacket, he plays guitar and won't talk to anyone. He's a misfit.

#misfit #outcast #social class #school #individual

When I say *misfit*, I'm talking about the fact that some of us just never found a way to fit in *at all*, from the get-go, all through our evolving lives, including in the present tense. I'm talking about how some of us experience that altered state of missing any kind of fitting in so profoundly that we nearly can't make it in life. We serially flounder, or worse, we drown in our inabilities or mistakes, or even worse—since I'm old enough to understand that sometimes some of us don't make it at all—we give up. Love and peace to the star stuff that carries those misfits we have lost too soon.

But I'm not here to draw pity.

Misfits, from my point of view, are everything. The world needs us. Here is the story of why.

• • •

I'd say I'm a misfit partly because of things that happened to me, and partly from things that come from the inside out. Hardwiring, if you will.

You see, some of us do life weird or wrong, or we do weird or wrong things in life. Some of us flunk out or go to jail or rehab or lose husbands or wives or children or houses or all the money. But the thing is, we don't all surrender or disappear, though some of us do. Lost secular angels. Some of us manage to invent bodies, voices, and lives worth living even though we don't fit in to the normative socius.

In our present tense, the older I get, the more I think that the social scripts we inherit along the way telling us who to be and how to fit in are bunk. The best we seem able to do is barely navigate those scripts, usually badly, like a bunch of mammals using their oars backward.

In fact, when I talk about "misfittery," what I hear most often is "oh, everyone is a misfit." And I know what people mean. In some ways, we all want to kind of "claim" the space of misfit, because let's face it, life is hard and weird and unfair and everyone, no exceptions, gets dosed once in a while. While I understand what people mean when they say that, I also think there is something important that only some of us have experienced that might help the rest of us get by, if our stories could be amplified.

I also understand the "anti-label" contingent. But I want to talk about the ways in which stepping into my misfittery, standing up inside it, and understanding it as a way of being and seeing in the world, saved my goddamn life.

Some of us have a point of view forged from both our experiences as well as our continued inability to enter culture, relationships, language, and social organization—the way we group ourselves in relationships, families, and communities—like other people. And there are a lot of us. Legions of us. For once I'd like to tell the story from our point of view, rather than from the projections and categories and DSM designations and false fictions society has made of us. The fallen, the broken, the abused, the recovering, the ex-cons, the vets, the survivors, the introverted, the not quite right: We are not your enemy. We are not something to be embarrassed about. We are not lesser or failed.

If you are a misfit, my hope is that you will see yourself reflected in these pages—from my story and the story of our fellow misfits. I've spoken with people who have figured out how to stand up inside their different ways of doing things, at the edges of culture. I hope to remind you that the edges of culture are exactly where new and beautiful meanings are generated. The edges help hold the center together. The edges are frontiers. The stories from other misfits in this book are here alongside mine to remind us all that we are not alone. We are always a part of one another—just like a conglomerate rock carrying sediments of earth from all over the world.

If you do not identify as a misfit, my hope is to illuminate the vital lessons we misfits have to share. We live in your periphery, right next to you every day of your life. We have ideas and innovations and heart to lend, but you'd have to learn to see us differently, on our own terms, and we'll all have to ask ourselves "how do our stories forge useful tributaries that might contribute to the human community?"

Here is a list we can at least begin with. Misfits know how to see mistakes and weirdness differently. We are differently sighted. We can see portals where other people see roadblocks.

Misfits are remarkably good at invention, reinvention.
Innovation in the face of what other people might see as failure.
We are resilient; we don't just survive, we invent how to thrive.
Misfits know how to help others because we are not driven by
some fiction of American excellence forged through ego and
competition—our egos are shot to shit, which helps us recognize
that it's our hands we need to extend, not our egos. We are not
frightened by otherness. Misfits transform fear and anger and
grief into expression rather than destruction—we give something
of value to the rest of culture rather than succumbing to our own
misery, particularly when those around us recognize our value.
Misfits know how to resist the homogenizing narratives of culture since we live at the edges. We help culture find new shapes.
We hold the center from the edges, we guard the perimeter.

There is nothing wrong with us. We are the rest of you. We
are useful to our culture and more; we have specific skills born
of resistance, reinvention, and resilience that are vital to human
existence. Put slightly differently, if we could all learn to see what
misfits see, that is, that so-called mistakes, failures, oddball
traits, and vulnerabilities are actually beautiful new roads to
creativity and social organization, we just might be able to begin
to redefine who we are and how we treat one another in a way that
does not celebritize some people while disappearing others.

We have voices.
We have bodies.
We have stories.

1 Not All Hope Comes from Looking Up

Aspiration gets stuck in some people. It's difficult to think "yes" or "up" when all you know is how to hold your breath and wait for horror to pass.

There is indeed a relationship between hope and misfittery, but it doesn't come from looking up, or rising, or climbing. Some misfits are drawn to the outside of things because they feel best when they feel different. But others of us were born through dirt and mud, trauma and violence. To forge hope, we had to invent it at ground zero.

Not all misfits are born up and through violence, but large numbers of us are.

Before I talk about trauma though, I'd like to take a moment to recognize the fact that at least some misfits emerge from happy families, from supportive environments, from lives and worlds that, at least from the outside, appear to be relatively stable. The girl who begins to carve lines into her arms, faint enough not to get caught, deep enough to bring tears to her eyes, but only when she's alone. She wears them like wrong bracelets in front of everyone. The boy who begins to adorn each wrist with bangles—more and more bangles—enough bangles to make his arms ring—just because he loves the sound they make when he reaches up to twirl his locker combination. Ally Sheedy in *The Breakfast Club*. Her glorious dandruff decorating her drawing with perfect snow. Those kids and teens who veer away from the central be-like-everyone-else path, those beautiful creatures forging weird little roads into the unknown, they remind us that beauty doesn't always come from mirroring the universal. It can also come from the weird on its way to becoming original and transformational.

Still, I've noticed from the stories fellow misfits tell me that many of our life paths run from rough beginnings. Perhaps it is true, or true enough, that trauma figures in our lives in a way that disfigures our understanding of the world and others. My colleagues in other disciplines have certainly told me enough stories over the years to support that idea—in psychology, sociology, anthropology. Then again, the older I get, the more I'm left feeling like trauma touches everyone in the end.

• • •

Here is a scene I've been writing and rewriting most of my adult life. It seems pivotal to my experience—like if I could just truly and finally figure one of these origin scenes out, I'd know something about life and how to live it. The setting is an ordinary kitchen in the 1970s. The scene is an ordinary argument between my parents. There were so many arguments they became normal even as I never stopped being terrified. I simply learned to endure, which left me with something akin to PTSD in the face of male anger as an adult. My sister's strategy was disassociation, and she was an expert at it, I'll tell you. I became an expert at taking it. Some people will understand that.

I'm eight. I'm sitting at the kitchen table. My sister is sixteen. She's washing dishes. My mother is sitting at the table with me. My father is in the doorway between the kitchen and the living room. My father and mother are both smoking and drinking coffee. The house smells like nicotine and caffeine and anger and child fear. I can see my sister's back, the motion of her forearms as she makes circular soapy patterns on each dish and places them one at a time—painstakingly slowly—into the dishwasher. At the zenith of their argument, both of them yelling, my father's voice the low-rage baritone of a rage-o-holic and my mother's the singsong screech of a Southern drawl, my mother stands up and slams her coffee mug on the table. Those big, extra-thick off-white ceramic coffee mugs. Coffee goes everywhere. Some splashes onto my hand, and it's hot, but I don't make a sound. Everyone is wearing bathrobes. My mother walks past my sister toward the other end of the kitchen, on her way to exit through the other doorway, and my father—who once had a walk-on tryout with the Cleveland Indians—hurls his mug at the wall, missing my mother's head by a centimeter. The bottoms of those extra-thick off-white ceramic coffee mugs are dark.

Nothing moves.

We are in the eye of a hurricane that does not come every season, but every other day, relentlessly.

There are so many ways to read this scene once I put it on the page. For one thing, what was my sister thinking?

What did my mother think?

What did he think, coming so close to her head with that powerful arm, that could-have-been-an-athlete arm?

Did anyone love their children in that moment, or any of the other endless moments? Or does love have nothing to do with it?

The hole in the wall remained for a very long time.

What I'm saying is that this moment is one in a series of paradigmatic scenes in my memory. Misfits, we all have such scenes in our memories. It is nowhere near the worst thing that happened to me, or my sister, or my mother with my father. In that house. But it rises up like an image that won't die. Sometimes I think everything about who we were and who we all became has its origins in moments like that.

Hope was nothing about that scene.

In place of hope, underneath my terror, which I had my entire childhood, was something else. That something else was the ability to endure, to stay quiet like a still animal close to the ground, and perhaps something even more important, the art of waiting for the right moment to act. I was, without knowing it, building a form of agency. I was, I know now, learning the art of agency in the eye of a storm, the art of understanding energies, the art of understanding that everything in life—violence to be sure but also everything else—is energy.

In my house, my father's rage incarcerated my mother, my sister, and me. His abuse threaded through our bodies, through our language, through every experience we could imagine, until that abuse seemed like part of everyday life. That's an important idea to consider. People who come from abuse or trauma or poverty don't exactly know how to see it in the world when they leave home and become adults, if they make it that far. You want to know why? It's familiar. So familiar we cannot recognize it. What I mean is, you can escape an abusive household, for example, and then step right into different abusive situations out in the world because they look and feel like something we are good at; it's what we know how to do. We gravitate toward the familiar. Couple that with the fact that our media representations and media realities are supersaturated with violence, trauma, and socioeconomic struggle as entertainment, and, well, there's no seeing to see, is there? So what we become experts at is endurance. We can, so to speak, take it. We're like Purple Heart combat veterans of a unique domestic and social variety. But it may be more accurate to call us ghost people who are a little haunted and always in danger of being dragged under . . . by depression, or fear, or failure, or our unusual relationship to reality.

I can imagine the terrible macro version of my micro story. Consider for a moment the legions of refugees fleeing the wars we've made worldwide: How will they fit into not only new countries, but also the stories we tell ourselves about identity and unity? I worry about them the same way I worry about individuals escaping violence in our own communities. In fact, considering our current administration's openly racist, homophobic, sexist, and xenophobic rhetoric and policy plans, there is an urgent crisis at hand: How will we tell the story of ourselves in America in a way that does not directly harm the most vulnerable among us? Who do we want to be?

But I'm sure even reading this you can see another side to the story I am telling about people born of difficulty. The broken side of coming from violence, war, abuse, trauma, or poverty. Misfits, we're also always expecting the fist, or the transgression, or the betrayal, or the bomb, or any one of a hundred smaller forms of violence. Even when they're not there. We carry with us the intense stare of someone who is ready at any moment to scrap to the death or surrender unto death—two sides of the same game— which can, in some cases, make us seem too quickly defensive or cranky or hard to work with or be around. We're often hard cases. In school, at jobs, in relationships.

And yet.

What if there is something else inside there, something of value?

Several events in my life have caused the traditional definition of hope to be sucked out of my body. I'm not saying I'm proud of this, but it just happened. For me, what became important in moments of trauma or despair or fear was learning to breathe differently. The word *aspiration* has a breathing sense to it. It dawned on me that we have to breathe and to find reasons to stay alive on our own terms.

●　　●　　●

There were two otherworlds that saved my life.

Swimming and art.

It's no great mystery why the swimming pool was my secular salvation. Four to six hours every day but Sunday I could leave the hell of home and enter the waters with other bodies. I could belong to something larger than myself that didn't involve a father or a godhead. And in the water, my mind freed itself. From the age of six to the day I left home for college, the only time I felt like my body and life were mine happened in chlorinated pools all over the country.

The otherworld I could escape into was art. I believe in art the way other people believe in God. I'm not trying to be dramatic here. It's just true. I have found reasons to breathe again by living in communities of people who choose self-expression over self-destruction. It's another way to form hope, without hierarchizing it so that you're looking up toward a father, or a god, or someone smarter or more famous or more heroic than you. I mean sure, that's one way to find inspiration, but it doesn't work on all of us. Our hope happens between ordinary people inventing their own ways of doing things. It's a lateral definition of hope, one emerging from the edges of things, where you just need to find each other, and you need to stand up and not leave each other hanging.

I found my story inside books and movies and paintings and music. I found my fellow sufferers, sure, my fellow weirdos and outcasts and misfits, but what I also found were stories of survival and beauty.

•   •   •

The first time I met my friend Sean Davis, we had a beer to-gether in Troutdale, Oregon, near the community college where we both had jobs. We talked about how community colleges are like petri dishes of America. Each classroom speckled with people who might not choose to sit next to the person they are near were it not for the fact that everyone needs to learn to read, write, and think critically. I'd already read Sean's great book *The Wax Bullet War*. So I already knew that "on September 12, 2001, a year and a half after finishing his military service, Sean Davis strolled into the Oregon National Guard's recruiting office and re-enlisted."[2] I already knew he came home with a Purple Heart, but also PTSD. What I learned sitting with him drinking that beer is that Sean is a father, a teacher, and an artist, and that his commitment to helping others is bigger than the Pacific Ocean. This is the story he told me:

From an early age I felt pushed to the margins because of how young my parents were when they had me (sixteen and eighteen), coming from a broken home, being the poor kid, and just ending up strange. At first being a misfit was very difficult for me. As a kid I felt sorry for myself all the time because of it, but as I grew into a man I realized that growing up a misfit was a positive aspect in my life. It was freeing. I was given a free peek behind the curtain in some weird way. I came to realize how hard it was for everyone to fit in, how difficult it was to maintain facades, and how lucky I was that I didn't have to be that way. The hardest part of it all was to find my feet. Confidence isn't an easy thing for the misfit, but once you find it, you can turn being one into a force. Now, it's my steadfast belief that history is made by the misfits.

Since I can remember, I've been responsible for someone. My first brother was born when I was two, my second brother when I was four. I looked out for them through an abusive parent, relatives' homes, poverty, school, the trailer parks, everywhere until they grew up. Then I had kids before I even grew up, and I raised them.

Then I was a leader in the military. Responsibility wasn't a choice; it was just always there. I say this because I believe to be a misfit, in how we're using the term, you need to have something in your core that keeps you going. I could have easily fallen into drugs, crime, or just stayed in a dead-end job ignorant of my own silent desperation. So yeah, when I was little I didn't choose to be different. As I get older it seems like it might be more of a choice, but I think it's ingrained, a learned behavior from a lifetime of experience fueled by something deeper that will always be a part of me. I think the real choice is choosing to be proud of who I am instead of ashamed for being different.

When I was a kid I tried very hard to fit in for a long time. I remember being in my room studying library books on cars. I really didn't care about cars, but the other boys in my school did. So I tried my best to care about them too. I would memorize the names and years made, the body styles, facts about the engines. I did this for days. Finally, I felt confident enough about it to enter a conversation on the way to school. An old truck passed the bus and I listed off every fact in the encyclopedia about Ford Falcons, Plymouth Valiants, and Chevy Novas. In the end the kids I tried to fit in with just thought I was so much weirder for my efforts. I think that is a microcosm of the plight of misfits.

My dad was very abusive when he was drunk. When sober he always, I mean always, had a book in his hand when he wasn't working. The difference between drunk and sober Dad was blaringly apparent. He's the guy who would knock my tooth out or break my nose (did both before I was eight), then apologize for Mr. Hyde the next morning. I mean sincerely apologize, tears and all. Physical abuse wasn't all he did when he was drunk. He robbed a liquor store with me and my brother in the car, he'd write bad checks, steal other people's rent money, fight all the time, crazy shit. He went to rehab a dozen times maybe. I say this because my two brothers and I said we'd never take a drink or do a drug because we saw what it did to Dad. We were convinced one sip of alcohol or one hit of a drug turned a person into a raving lunatic. My youngest brother, to this day, still doesn't drink. In fact, he doesn't even let the dentist give him painkillers. He won't take anything that can alter his consciousness.

I didn't drink or smoke until I was twenty-one and in the military. I joined the infantry in the early nineties; it was where you put poor black kids, poor Mexicans, poor white trash. It was really hard work so we played really hard too. There weren't any nondrinkers and very few nonsmokers in the regular army infantry. Of course, I didn't do drugs. We were piss tested every one to three months without warning, but I did drink myself black several times. It was a kind of test of manhood. Stupid for sure, but we did it. Burned through women, too. That was just as much of a vice.

I'd never had self-confidence being a beaten kid, not until the military, and it was a strange kind of confidence. The root of it came from not giving a fuck if you lived or died. I'm sure you know what I'm talking about. Imagine a young kid, in the best shape of his life, training to kill people and blow shit up for his job, with a very destructive drinking habit fueled by the macho need to defy death.

Then throw in a divorce, a revolution in Haiti, a war in Iraq, Hurricane Katrina, Dad dying, PTSD . . .

In 2005 on New Year's, I made a resolution to either stay drunk all year or drink myself to death. I made it to Easter Sunday. Every day, if I didn't black out before dark, I'd go to the Belmont Inn and get into fistfights in the back with random people. Showed up to army drill drunk. Burned through women again. Bad person.

I'd say I turned it around that Easter. I woke up next to a woman I didn't know with bad tattoos. Thought about how much I was like Dad. And that's when I started painting and writing again. It was a question of identity, I think. I didn't have to be the army guy anymore, or the beat kid, or the self-destructive asshole.

I really think that's where my life started. Before that, my life was being lived by people I hardly knew or wanted to remember.

When I read Kurt Vonnegut for the first time I felt like a door opened. A really big door. A door to a life I never even imagined possible. The first time I wrote a story I felt my own heart beating differently. The first time I painted a painting I understood that I was much more than my dad—because I could feel possibilities for expression all around me. Now I teach other people how to write in the hopes that they can find expression too.

My friend Sean Davis? He wound up running the American Legion/Veterans of Foreign Wars Post 134 in Portland on Alberta Street. In addition to the pool table, he organized literary readings of all sorts there, an LGBTQ bingo night, and a weekly discussion group for vets. He has also ushered several vets toward artistic practice, helping to produce and stage original plays and operas in addition to writing their own stories and poems. He has an MFA in creative writing. He teaches college English courses in writing and literature at more than one community college. In the summers he fights fires. He ran for mayor and not only did exceptionally well, but also changed the tenor and discourse of the entire election.

Sean Davis earned a Purple Heart.

That's an incredibly high honor. Maybe even the highest. A truly heroic accomplishment. But I think the more important heart is in his commitment to other people in his community, no matter where he is, no matter what he is doing, being a misfit gloriously and without apology. He excels partly because he did not fit in. He knows how to help other people exist and find something culture doesn't: Self-esteem. Worth. Even when your past or your culture says you are nothing.

Our life stories? We made them up from nothing.

So one kind of misfit is the child who grew up and through one kind of violence or another, and what we have to give is this: We can endure. We know how to breathe differently in a crisis, with calm and presence. And even as we felt none or were robbed of it along the way, we know how to illuminate a path to self-worth based on helping others, based on recognizing that you belong to something besides the violence around you.

2 Coloring (and Sometimes Living) Outside the Lines

It's not that I completely reject rules or good citizenship. It's that I find more self-worth at the edges of things, at the so-called outlaw or agitator seams: the places where people who do not quite fit in find themselves breaking rules or making noise.

Most misfits struggle against the story that's expected of them. You know, the cultural scripts of good citizenship that come at us in life: how to be a woman, how to be a man, how to be successful at jobs/relationships/life, how to be happy, how to love, how to marry, how to fit into society. Misfits chafe at the stories placed in front of them or on top of them because nothing about our experiences in life matches up with the traditional or mainstream story line. We hit those story lines of identity and social organization head-on, and the subsequent wreck either destroys us or inspires us to forge original paths.

For example, though I was briefly raised Catholic, it did not work on me to go to church and pray, or to believe in a god that would let priests fondle children. It did not work on me to obey my father as the head of my family, since he was the origin of our abuse. It did not work on me to tell me to go to school and work hard, because it had exactly zero impact on my life at home. It did not work on me to be punished, nor did it work to be praised, since in my house those two things had been monstrously conflated. Loving my mother didn't help, because loving as she was, she also began to drink, and thus she created her own drowning waters. It did not, in any way, help me to imagine believing in something like a hero who would come and save me. No one was going to come and save me. This is a fact that some of us had to figure out how to live with, or not. That's the thing about misfits. We can't fit the stories of who we are supposed to be, nor can we fit the stories that society makes for us to be okay in the world, so we have to invent our own stories or die trying. You might say we invent whole alternative belief systems.

If there's one phrase that I should probably tattoo on my forehead it is this: *I'm not the story you made of me.* The more people I can persuade to hold that mantra, the more I'll have been of good use in my life. We don't have to accept the stories we inherit, the ones that tell us who we're supposed to be. We can stand up and say no at any point, even if we've been saying yes our entire lives. It's never too late. We can always reject the story placed on top of us, and we can always revise and destroy one story and restore another. It's a never-ending possibility.

In some ways, my body story, or what I think of as the stories of our experiences that we are all walking around physically carrying, could be read as a resistance narrative. I remember my first day of kindergarten in Washington State quite vividly. My mother drove me to school, walked me to the classroom, and left me sobbing by the coatracks. The teacher nearly dragged me to a table of strangers and sat me down hard. I continued

my wailing. The teacher raised her voice and brought her hand
down hard on the table in front of me. By that time I was crying
so hard I was hiccupping. So she marched me back over to the
coatracks for something like a time-out, the other kids staring
at me like I was an alien the entire time, all of them silent and
obedient.

I remember how the coats smelled. They smelled like outside.
I remember all the colors and textures of those coats like it was
yesterday. Corduroy and navy-blue wool. Red ski parkas and
a white raincoat. The coats calmed me. I couldn't make this
sentence then, but the feeling was in me already: I have more
in common with these coats than I do with those creatures over
there at the tables.

I was a hard-core introvert thrown into my first social experience. Who knows—maybe I was even on the spectrum, as we
say now. Sometimes I wonder if I've just masterfully passed all
of these years.

When I stopped crying and hyperventilating, the teacher
marched me back to the table where five or so kids sat quietly
drawing trees. She put a piece of paper in front of me and told
me to draw a tree. When she walked back to her desk, I calmly
selected a giant purple crayon and scrawled a giant purple line
across the entire table as hard as I could.

Maybe I wanted to get out of that room. Maybe "school" terrified me, as nearly everything outside my home did at that time.

Or maybe my purple line was a cry for help, as in, *My house is
not safe, my life terrifies me, can't anyone hear me, I'm crying as
hard as I can.*

Sometimes kids make their own language before you teach them how to make words and sentences.

The first time I consciously experienced that I did not fit the story around me was on an elementary school playground. I've tried to write this scene a hundred times, and it always comes out a little wrong. You'll see why. The story doesn't quite fit our idea of ourselves. Four girls playing four square. Me the only one in jeans and a checkered cowboy shirt with snap buttons. My hair and eyebrows white like an albino's. Tall gangly boy from what used to be called the special ed zone of the school—the place where kids who were basically different from us, or so we were told—crosses the territory between our segregated playgrounds. The playgrounds were next to one another, and yet separate. I don't see him at first but the other three girls do, they scatter and scream, and before I quite see what's what, he grabs me, bends me backward Hollywood style, and plants a big slobbery kiss on my lips. Then he just walks away.

In the world of cruelty and playground girls, we're both instantly marked. I become the girl with the too-white hair who the special ed kid attacked. Even though I'm really just me standing there, my face hot, my mind too many marbles colliding. Even though he's just the kid who crossed playgrounds briefly. I watch him walk away and recede. There is a tiny bit of boy slobber on my chin. I stretch my tongue to find it. Even at that age I know he did the Hollywood bend back move perfectly.

I didn't think "I'm a misfit" as a sentence in that moment, nor did I think that other kid who kissed me was a misfit, but I did feel the air around me become a vacuum, and I had the strangest impulse to follow him. I wanted to follow him away from the playground girls who I could never mimic enough to be accepted. I wanted to follow him to whatever world he inhabited that would take me away from the screaming girls, but maybe more than that, away from the secret I was carrying around—abuse lived at my house. Didn't that make me different? If I followed him, would someone finally notice?

But I did not follow him. I just stood there, alone and confused. Those four square girls didn't let me play with them for the rest of the year. I stopped going out to the playground at all. I took clarinet lessons with the only black kid at my school, and during recess we stayed inside to practice.

So yeah.

I'm the kid who got hit in the face during dodgeball.

I'm the kid who peed her pants in sixth grade.

I'm the teen who wore overalls and Converse high tops all through middle school, the one who ate lunch in our designated locker hallway sitting on the floor with my one and only friend.

I'm the young woman who slept around, who found drugs and alcohol and sex to be portals out and away from my reality. I'm the one who got arrested and sent to rehab or jail. All of it was better than living in my father's house.

That boy? The one who was in so-called special ed? He became a concert pianist in Seattle.

I have no idea what became of the four square girls.

The first time I admitted to myself as an adult that I was never going to smoothly fit in with everyone else happened when my daughter died. Unlike some women who seem to eventually emerge from that dark underwater world, I lingered. Not only did I linger inside grief and depression for years, but early on I did something some people from the outside might regard as nutty. I stopped going to work. I stopped going to college classes. I began sleeping underneath an overpass rather than inside a house. Something about the ghost world of homelessness made more sense to me than the rest of the so-called well-adjusted world of people did. Maybe I was looking for something. Something I lost besides my daughter. What I'm saying is that my actions had a logic, even if that logic isn't easy to see.

What I found underneath the overpass were former doctors and lawyers. Straight-A students who took some drastic turn or fall. One former Olympic athlete and several teachers and bankers and yes, a CEO; his wife was killed in an accident involving two drunk drivers—one of whom was him. Yes, I also found alcoholics and junkies and ex-cons, but they were also combat veterans, single mothers, engineers, pilots, and virtuoso musicians. In other words, what I found underneath the overpass was us.

Homeless people are some of the most heroic misfits on earth because they start out as us, and they travel to the darkest edges of being and survival. If only we could get to the point where we understood and welcomed the knowledge and experience they've gleaned on our behalf. If we could learn how to listen to homeless people and respect their experiences and make a place for them in our culture, if only we could admit that they are the other side of each and every one of us, and that we need them and what they know in order to not lose track of what being human really means, well, wouldn't that be something?

What I learned from that intensely educational period of my life is that one kind of misfit is the person who suffers abuse or trauma and doesn't transcend it in the socially hoped-for way. We take a wrong turn or go deeper down. That's often looked at like a failure, but sometimes I wonder. I've learned things by taking the wrong turn or going down deeper that I could not have learned any other way. The other thing I learned is that misfitting is partly caused by circumstance, and partly something that happens on the inside of a person, as when I wanted to walk out of one reality and into another, which has now happened several times in my life. Misfits know a great deal about how to step out of one reality and into another. Sometimes it's the thing that saves your life.

●　　●　　●

Where I work, at a community college in Oregon, the student body is made up of single mothers and ex-cons, people just out of rehab or recently relapsed, people living in their cars, people with two or three or even four jobs who are trying to feed their kids and not go nuts, people on mental health meds and people who barely speak English and people who are the first individuals to dare to dream that a life of the mind might not be as crazy as it sounds. Migrant workers and gas station attendants. Middle-aged people who lost their jobs and now have to reinvent themselves. Former sex workers and dropouts and screwups. And yes, former or even current homeless people.

There are outspoken Republicans sitting next to righteous tree huggers. Business majors next to potheads. Gay men next to football players. Or football players who are gay men next to boys whose granddads were in the KKK. Pregnant women next to former gang members. Straight-A students next to never-passed-a-class-in-their-lives folks. Transgender men or women next to uber-conservative Christians. A veteran who lost both legs next to a woman who spent the previous week at a hospital on a psych hold.

Though there are still mostly white people, because it is Oregon after all, there are also African Americans, Asian Americans, and Latino Americans, as well as people from the other two Americas—Central and South. There are Ukrainians and Filipinos and Somalis. There are Vietnamese people and Koreans and American Indians. And more.

In a way, I teach in the classrooms of American broken-down dreams. And yet in these classrooms, America is secularly born again, the classroom of no choice who you sit next to, no way to separate yourself from otherness, no way to get out of the room unless you agree to be together for a while. It's like a petri dish of who we are and where we are at, teaching and learning at a community college.

Last year I attended a legal hearing designed to determine whether a student in one of my classes should go back to prison or be placed in a special program that would allow him to con-tinue going to classes part-time. I'd already bailed him out when he got arrested again, whether or not that was the right thing to do. I'd already written to the district judge on his behalf. I'd already provided evidence of his mind and talent.

In the classroom, this man wrote essays about how hard it is to move from gang life in Mexico to regular life in Oregon. His essays centered on a dream he has, a dream of starting a program for gang youth. You know, like a rec center, some classes, some visiting artists and writers and business leaders. He said the gang life just relocated itself in microversions once Latino men got here, and he wanted to spend the rest of his adult life trying to interrupt that motion. His essays were passionate. Publishable.

I worked with this man for two years—I mean he was in my classroom for two years. I watched him inspire people without even knowing he was doing it. He just told the truth. For two years what he worked on the hardest was where to put rage, and I'd convinced him the page would hold it.

He became more and more articulate.

And then he became eloquent.

And then he became a person who could truly effect change, his beautiful pages rising like birds in the sky.

So when he asked me to speak on his behalf at his hearing and to write to the district judge, I did. Enthusiastically. Repeatedly. But his past kept coming up. Getting bigger. Harder to explain. Nothing I said or did seemed to matter. Not my PhD, not my twenty-eight years of teaching experience, not my passionate plea about the excellence and eloquence of his writing. In the end we were just two people who had both broken the law, been arrested, and been incarcerated.

I have a past too.

I got another chance.

He had to go back—to that other institution.

The reasoning used regarding why he had to go back is mind-numbingly idiotic, even if we call it "the law." Now he's writing essays from prison. I don't know if he'll lose heart. But I would understand if he did.

Another student I'm working with is currently living in her car. She did two tours of duty in the Middle East and came home to her daughter—minus the use of her right hand and half of her face. The one-bedroom apartment she was living in raised the rent from $400 a month—which she could just barely manage as a single mother with a disability and PTSD—to $950 a month. With sixty days' notice. Which is legal in Oregon.

Boom. Like a bomb going off. Homeless.

The wait at the social services office where she can get help is ninety days. The wait at the women's shelter right now is twenty-eight days, and she's not as high on the intake list as the women who are being beaten and in immediate danger. One day she's in my American literature class hoping to become a teacher. The next she's living in her car, her daughter passed off every day to a different friend, which only works sometimes. I couldn't live with knowing that, so I found her some immediate help, but here's the thing: I know I can't help them all, and the choices we are making as a country that ever decrease funding for programs that might help disenfranchised people every day of our lives will only mean that more people who can't make it— like the walking wounded—will show up.

Where are the Purple Hearts for the men, women, and children who have managed to endure?

Listen, I'm not telling you this to highlight my efforts. I'm telling you this to highlight how much we are all pieces of each other.

I'm like them.

You might look at some of my life events as a list of indicators of trouble ahead:

Between the ages of four and ten I ate non-nutritive things. Like dirt and paper and small stones and pennies. The clinical term for this is pica disorder.

As a kid, I missed quite a few developmental stages—I didn't speak out loud for a good long time, much later than child psychologists and doctors suggest, I wet my pants through sixth grade, and I couldn't ride a bike until I was twenty-five.

I am the daughter of an abusive father whose house I had narrowly escaped with my life.

I have two *epically* failed marriages under my belt.

I've flunked out of college not once, but twice, and maybe even a third time.

I've been through one episode of drug rehab and two brief stints incarcerated. I've also been homeless.

I'm not a deviant. Or a loser. Or a criminal.

I'm someone who "missed" fitting in.

Perhaps that list is mapping out the fault lines of a life, but can't we admit that everyone on the planet carries fault lines in their lives, so isn't there a way to see the echo effect of all our vulnerabilities inside the stories of our lives? Our vulnerabilities make us most human, most beautiful, most like each other.

What was mostly wrong with me when I took my nosedive was that my daughter died the day she was born, and when that piled up on top of where I came from (abuse, addiction), I just didn't know how to live with that story.

But my life, like a lot of other people's lives, also has interesting positive mutations in addition to mistakes. I have a PhD, I'm a tenured professor, and I've published seven books. I've received prestigious awards for my writing; I've stood on magical stages of various sorts.

You want to know what makes me different from the people I am telling you about? Nothing.

Which is to say that I have been like the people I am talking to you about, and some of you are too, and we are all standing in rooms next to one another, and the one language we can all understand, if we remember to, is empathy. Compassion. No one is perfect. No one got where they are without occasionally falling to pieces. Maybe it's time we admit that we need all of us for any of us to make it.

We may be misfits, but that's only if you look at us from the wrong angle. Turn us even slightly, and we brighten like the phenomenal colors inside a kaleidoscope.

Now more than ever we have to let go of the idea that categories such as business and industry and education and government and law enforcement and medicine and technology and the arts are separate and isolated from one another. Now more than ever we have to figure out how to braid our languages before it's too late.

Yes, I understand these are sad stories. So let me tell you about someone who started out sad and shot the moon. This woman started out in a series of foster homes. Her story is so bleak I'm not even going to tell it. You already know how bleak. Even though we don't like to look at it, we know. Passed from home to home. From bad to worse. Her body the word for it. For her entire childhood. I'm not ashamed to tell you, I'm surprised she came to my classroom alive.

But here's the thing. When she showed up in my classroom, what she had in her was a passion for three things: math, science, and poetry. Like a strange new species. She graduated from community college with a transfer degree, which, for those of you who don't know, is like a ticket to ride—a realistic form of mobility. To a misfit, that's a golden ticket. She went on to get a degree at Portland State University. From there she went to MIT. From there she did postdoctoral work at Yale. Now she works at the European Organization for Nuclear Research, also known as CERN. I hear her first book of poetry is forthcoming.

Everything against her. Nothing stopping her. Except all the people who tried.

Sometimes I think about her when I'm blue. I look up at the stars in the night sky and think about her poems and I wonder if she is inventing new cosmologies, re-storying the whole world.

I hope with all my heart that my Latino friend—for our relationship is no longer that of teacher and student—keeps writing his essays from prison. He is a part of me. I hope with my whole body that he does not lose heart. I believe in him.

I hope that my single-mother friend doesn't fall through the cracks. I hope she doesn't let go of her dream to study and teach world literature in another country. I hope our country doesn't let her down.

What I hope most of all is that we all begin to recognize how much we have to change in the face of our current culture. I hope we all learn to admit that we carry the trace of one another, that all our languages may yet reach one another, even inside our differences.

·   ·   ·

I first met my friend Mary J. Thompson as a student in my women's studies class at Mt. Hood Community College. I knew right away that she was different, but until I read her writing, I didn't know how. Her story then, and knowing her now, helps me remember to never give up on anyone. Ever. Because we never know when the person standing next to us might actually save a life, simply by sharing their story.

For me, misfits are those of us who in some way grew up without seat belts, having to come to our own beliefs of the world and our ideas of selfhood. Either because of family dysfunction or by being different in some way, societal norms did not fit or deemed us unworthy. Or we could not live societal norms because our sense of self was mutated. All of which left us being different and paving our own roads. For me, sometimes those roads were dead ends or rough but they were always my own.

My misfit story began in 1956. I was the tenth child born into a family that did not want or need any more children. Both my parents were mentally ill and could not love their children in many identifiable ways. I was born mixed, which in the 1950s was a big deal that left me treated differently by teachers and social workers.

My family resembled Lord of the Flies *more than a family. Isolation from society and within my family was how I grew up. I was alone with only the animals, my fantasies, and books to communicate with. My only physical affection from people came from sexual abuse. Emotional, physical, and sexual abuse was the order of the day and when it wasn't there I steeled myself for its return.*

Coping skills got me through for many years but they left me unable to fit in anywhere in any meaningful way. My family did not bond with one another. When I left home at thirteen I didn't just not miss them, they completely went out of my consciousness until I saw them again. The term for this is attachment disorder. It means that I did not attach at all to people around me or at times suffered from needs I did not understand. My sense of self was fractured into separate fragments of characters I designed as a child to cope with abuse. The term for this is dissociative identity disorder. It seemed to work for a long time until it didn't. My body and head were severed from each other, unable to communicate pain, sexuality, and a whole self. Sex abuse had left me promiscuous, but the separation of head from body removed the possibility of feeling anything positive from those interactions. Life's cues went unnoticed. I could not decipher danger or affection. So I often found myself in danger, unable to identify when people did *care about me.*

There were certain things that got me through and later gave me the ability to heal. I could see my family even though they did not see me—an ability I may have been born with. Even when they were hurting me I could see their faces and their humanity. I read a lot, which helped me acquire the understanding that I was not the only child who suffered. Books gave me new ways to interpret the world around me. They gave me more compassion. Stories from family and books gave me strength. In that family of violence I learned how to fight between times of hopelessness. Those moments when I stood up and fought back helped me have a sense that I could change things. I fought to survive. The fight itself changed and empowered me to not give up on myself. It was always okay to fight for others, but not having a clear sense of self and worth left me immobilized, often unable to stand up for myself.

Foster care made my self-alienation worse because it was dysfunctional too, in its own way, and I was placed in white homes where I felt completely at sea. The ability to walk away without a plan and have faith that something would happen served me well in getting out of those homes. There have been a few homeless periods in my life where I lived by wit. That lifestyle taught me how to ride the waves and keep going. Surviving homelessness takes creativity every day, facing many hurdles to stay safe and eat. I had a lot of short-term relationships and the longer ones with friends usually were trouble. I bounced out of college three or four times. Mental and physical disabilities would not let me free. Because I did not know how to be around safe people I picked people who did not care about me to be with. But I kept the ability to leave on a dime. Some of the things that happened, like being reoffended by family members, put me in a horrible mental state for years. This was the time I hurt myself because I must have deserved it all.

I got help on occasion from counseling but most of that did not help anything. One guy was good and I saw him for a couple years off and on. But the others made me feel like I was a victim and that doesn't help ever. I would get pissed and leave. Professionals at the time did not know what to do with me. Some people helped along the way, mostly the ones who just accepted me. What got me to start healing was getting safe and my basic needs met. Once that happened when I was older I set about healing. It is funny that it did not happen then. Maybe just talking to others helped, but when they tried to get me to have feelings like "normal" people I just felt more scarred.

Healing started to happen when I really started to help others. I did not set out to do that but it was put in front of me. At the same time I connected with my own native culture again and that helped me feel saner. I sat with the dying and it taught me a lot about life. I helped people in dire situations out by just trying to do the next right thing because I did not have a plan or know how to live. I made a decision to do what was put in front of me without knowing what a drastic decision that was. But I kept doing it. My children taught me how to love really and being with these other people did too.

Healing comes in spurts for me and when I went back to school as an elder to become a writer I entered into another one of those times. I could always see others, but in writing I began to see myself. I began to forgive myself. There is something about writing your own story from the position of observer that gave me new sight. It gave me empathy for who I had been and mistakes I had made. Writing helped me see the strength that had always been there but that I had discounted. All the things I went through have become strengths and experiences I can use for growth and being a better human being.

Mistakes I made that hurt people bothered me more than people hurting me. But those mistakes helped make me who I am because I did not pass them up. I looked at them directly. At first I thought it made me a horrid person. They hang with you more than successes do. But in actuality mistakes helped define me to myself. I knew what I did not want to be. I had no role models for who I did want to be. Mistakes promoted change in my life only because I took ownership of those mistakes and responsibility to change my behavior. At first that meant stopping self-destructive behavior but I hurt myself because I felt like crap. Later I realized I did not have to hurt myself because I too was a human being and not just the mistakes I made. A conscious life can come from evaluating ourselves. In that way of looking, people become better humans each day.

Writing helped me see that even though I was fearful throughout my life, I had kept going and done the hard things. I brought up the hard conversations with my family even when they threatened or belittled me. Each step was a step back into the self I was meant to be. When I was afraid enough to roll up in a ball and die I did not. Sometimes I think for many of us misfits it's like peeling away one finger at a time to get out of the ball we want to roll up into.

Sympathy helps no one and just leaves people feeling worse. In my life today when I meet people who are misfits like me, the best thing to do is help them get safe if they are not, give them a meal, and give them room to grow into who they need to be. I love seeing people get their voices and power back. I have helped people get off the streets, out of abusive relationships, and kids who were at risk. People need to be safe and feel safe and fed. Then it is not so much what we do but how we support others to become what they hope to be. Love and acceptance are the only real things we have to give of the most importance. But physical safety and needs are always primary. So in my life today I show up and have shown up in places like prisons or sweat lodges or any place and do or have done my best to be supportive of others' journeys.

When I was little I wanted to be like everyone else. Today I just want to be and enjoy my own misfit self—trying to be the best human I can be. I will never be like other people. I process things differently and live differently. The law still does not faze me and I see a difference between the law and justice. My desires are not for money or fame. Justice and compassion are what are important, along with trying to make some kind of positive difference in the world. I don't know if I will ever feel relationships or love like other people but I do know that my relationships engender deep thought and feeling inside me, and considering what I've been through and where I came from, I'd say that's worth something.

3 The Myth that Suffering Makes You Stronger

What a crock of shit.

In America, but likely other places, there's a ready-made story about suffering that has its roots in the Christ story. In it, suffering takes on mythical (or cinematic, depending on your point of view) proportions. From it, we are supposed to learn two things: 1. No one can possibly suffer like Christ suffers, so you know, suck it up, sister, because he died for YOU. 2. Through suffering one finds grace. You are closer to God inside states of suffering.

It's also at the core of most American mainstream novels, films, and television dramas.

Once the male partner of a female friend who was stricken with a very serious illness midtravel in Europe said the following to me: "She's suffering so terribly. I've never seen such grace." Yes, I understand what he meant. Yes, I understand that he was scared and grieving, that the woman he loved was very ill and he was beside himself. But the truth is that I instantly wanted to punch his face off his head. Her suffering, whatever it was, was hers. His story pissed me off. She was diagnosed with lupus. She was bedridden in a foreign country for quite some time. Lupus is lifelong, and also impacts how long the life will be.

Grace is not the word we should fall for.

What I'm getting at is, there's a mythology surrounding surviving suffering that can be inspiring to some, but can make others feel like they're suffering the wrong way.

• • •

I truly hate the "suffering makes you stronger" narrative. The truth is, suffering sucks and it can take you to a place of wanting to kill yourself, and there's nothing beautiful about that. Suffering is not a state of grace. The suffering model Mother Teresa speaks of is not the one that moves me: "Pain and suffering have come into your life, but remember pain, sorrow, suffering are but the kiss of Jesus—a sign that you have come so close to Him that He can kiss you."

Suffering, from my point of view, is about a real place in a real body where you face the other side of living. How you choose to understand that story probably determines how you're going to live the rest of your life. I feel kindred with fellow sufferers, not because they suffer, and not because of some absurd vortex of victimhood camaraderie, and not because sufferers are in a state of grace, but because they go on, they endure. And because sometimes, the sufferer reinvents themself—and this kind of reinvention is what misfits are so good at. Misfits not only know a great deal about alternate and varied definitions of suffering, but misfits are also capable of alchemizing suffering, changing the energy from one form to another.

I identify mightily with people who have been so lost they literally had to reinvent their own feet in order to make a move. My mother was born with one leg six inches shorter than the other; she had special built-up shoes made so that her limp would not be as apparent and her pain would lessen. It was my first understanding of difference, of not fitting in, of watching people look at her differently and treat her differently. Her shoes fascinated me as a child. I also wanted to grab her cane and hit several people over the head with it on occasion. My mother was in pain every day of her life. From her pain she reinvented a self. A woman who would win real estate awards as well as awards for walking door-to-door for the March of Dimes year after year. But her suffering was not beautiful. It was simply the fire from which her imagination was forged. I don't ever want to romanticize the story of suffering, because then you're just playing into making it a good story or a sellable story for a culture that wants to be entertained by your suffering.

Ew.

So let me tell you a different suffering story that cannot be corralled by a culture that asks you to process your suffering in ways that make you a good citizen in an ever-churning economy of productive people. The same culture that has developed the psychological and medical and pharmaceutical and self-help industries to keep you in an endless loop of need.

I've told you that my daughter died the day she was born. I am not the only person who has experienced the suffering that comes from such a loss. But I am one of those who is willing to stand up, tell the story out loud, admit that I have carried that profound loss, that birth-death crisis, for more than thirty years now. Here is the thing I want to say loudest of all: I haven't transcended anything. No great revelation has come my way. I haven't ascended into some magical wisdom. I haven't "moved on." At least not without her. My daughter I mean. And my suffering is not a state of grace. It's just a part of me. Like my heart.

When her birth-death first happened, here is what I did: I lost my marbles.

It did not happen instantly. For instance, at the hospital I could feel myself disintegrating a molecule at a time, but I didn't say anything. I sat in the hospital shower after the birth. I could hear the voice of my sister, loving, compassionate, present, though it sounded like it was moving through water. I could see the body and face of my first husband, slumped in a chair, not having any idea what to "do." His hands were everything about him. He was a phenomenal painter and a virtuoso on the guitar. His fingers were unusually long and beautiful. I think I stared at his fingers so hard and for so many days in a row, he became his hands, and I could live with that. I drank the water they gave me, though I didn't eat the food. I held my swaddled lifeless daughter several times. I kissed her, I cradled her, I sang to her. I let the nurses give me a hot towel "bath" in the bed the second night, which remains on my list of top five most phenomenal physical experiences of my life. I thought I might be dead, but the heated wet towels reminded my skin that I was in fact alive, even if I was deadened. I thus understood myself to be in a perfectly liminal space between life and death. By the time they released me and sent me home, I wasn't speaking at all, to anyone. And I wouldn't let a single human touch me. I felt . . . mammalian. Back to some animal past of pure instinct and wariness of everything around me. The hair on my legs and arms grew long, like white fur, which sometimes happens when someone stops eating.

At home, I wailed at irregular intervals.

My first husband—who I was already separated from—took me on night walks to a nearby cemetery that was a favorite place of mine. We'd sit on the ground with dead people and he'd throw a silver dollar into the air and we'd watch bats dive for it.

My emotions were bigger than my body, and thus, my mind slipped. Wavered. Traveled to some place I now understand is tantamount to psychosis, but at the time, it just seemed like I'd entered a room filled with night water.

It was my sister who brought me back to life, slowly, feeding me bits of saltine crackers to lure me back, and then one day an egg, and eventually, a milk shake. The milk shake made me smile.

It was my sister who stepped fully clothed into the shower with me when she would hear me sobbing . . . or maybe they were animal sounds, I don't know. I just know she held me tight like a mother would, and her clothes, I began to feel the texture of her clothes against my skin.

It took almost a year.

Partway through that first year, I did something unethical. I lied. I lied more than you can imagine. I went back to college, and I had a part-time job at a daycare center, which in retrospect may have been a tragic error. I lied to everyone who asked me about my daughter. I lied at work. I lied at school. I lied at the grocery store and the bus stop. I told anyone and everyone that she was alive, she was beautiful, such long eyelashes. I lied about where we were living, I lied about the classes I was barely attending, I lied about the baby shower no one ever gave me, I lied about breastfeeding and sore nipples and smelling like milk and pee. I'd throw my head back and laugh and say, "Motherhood!" What I'm telling you is that in the face of people who came toward me with their regular-person questions about my pregnancy and birth story, I broke into fictions because I could not make what happened come out of my mouth. My story didn't fit the other mothers' stories. Misfit.

My lying started out as me telling people I was staying at a friend's house, which was a story line that passed quite well. But I wasn't living with a friend. In the tapestry inside my head and heart a new weaving emerged that made a kind of "sense" given how it felt to be me. What it felt like to be me was that I was among the walking dead, and I lived at the bottom of a very dark ocean. A ghost person living in some sea wreckage. And so I gravitated toward other ghost people, at night, and I started sleeping under an overpass just at the edge of town, near a bus stop where buses would take me back to the normalcy of a college campus during the day.

I read books.

I wrote a paper or two.

I passed a test here and there.

I took showers in the women's locker rooms of the University of Oregon swimming pool, the same pool where I'd qualified for Junior Nationals at fourteen years old.

My daughter's death was so alive in me it felt like we were two people walking around. I mean she felt that present to me—like a second body. As present as when she swam her days and nights away inside the world of my belly. I drank every single day in incremental amounts. I "passed" in every sphere of regular life I entered, but I entered those spheres less and less, and spent more and more time under the overpass. I was never alone. My daughter was with me. Some people will understand this kind of ghost life. This kind of haunting, a haunting of the body, an inside-out reality. Some of us will carry the dead the rest of our lives.

I had a notebook in which I wrote pages and pages of crazy lady gibberish, or seeming gibberish. I read all kinds of books. Inside the books I again saw stories that I recognized, because, well, literature is filled with characters whose lives are so broken they can barely breathe. Literature is the land of the misfitted.

Inside that notebook filled with what may have looked to an outside observer like strange hieroglyphics, in between the lines, there were glimpses of actual stories. The stories were about strange girls filled with rage or love or art that came shooting out of them, almost violently. And as I stepped back toward the world, I saw that the lies I'd been telling weren't lies at all. They were precise fictions about living inside a woman's body, and the journey I'd just made to the bottom of an ocean, the journey to death and back. What other people called lies were actually portals to finding my ability to invent stories.

Ten years later the quality of my suffering took on a different form. My suffering became hunger. It felt like grief and loss gutted me and left a crater. After a while, instead of consuming me, the hole generated something living alongside the nothing: a very human kind of ache, the ache to hold something—anything—real.

In the place inside my body where my dead daughter carved out a hole, a new and all-consuming hunger was born. Nature abhors a vacuum; hunger comes from a kind of kinetic pressure in us, an animal want that might have made me jump off a bridge, but instead turned into a kind of furious creative drive. Hunger for ideas, hunger for sex, hunger for danger, hunger for risk. I read every book I could get my hands on, then I'd research the books the author had read and I'd read all of those. I slept with teachers, with students, with drunks and junkies, men and women, with anyone who had a glint of fire or danger in the corner of their eye. There wasn't a drug I wouldn't try. I attended my first BDSM party, armed with an invitation from my dear friend Paige, and found people who didn't need me to pass as anything but a ravaged body. I'd get high and ride my bike down to the rapids of the Willamette River and dive in and ride them with the other punks and street kids nuts enough to find that "fun." The fun of the death drive driving you.

What I no doubt do not need to explain is how dangerous my hunger and subsequent behavior were. That's a story line we are all trained to understand.

What I do want to explain is what my hunger was *generative* of. What looks from the outside like self-destruction isn't always so. The other side of destruction is always the possibility of self-expression. Creativity. The mistake we make with teens and young adults and broken adults is to forget that. All creativity has destruction as its other, just like the beyond beautiful dead infant I held in my arms. What I saw in literary books was a possible path from suffering and self-destruction to self-expression. I went back to the nutso gibberish I wrote down in that notebook under the overpass, and I began to cull the stories.

Once I started writing I never stopped. For this reason I would say that the death of my daughter and entering a real place called psychosis and being homeless were not just tragic. They were generative. Those experiences put writing into my hands.

Twenty years later the quality of the suffering took shape and form on pages. The girl I lost became the girl I found inside stories where girls nearly die but then don't, where girls with their hair on fire invent ways to save themselves, where girls who are incarcerated by family or violence or love or social norms break out of culture and into journeys no one has ever imagined before. What I'm saying is, the more I wrote, the more I understood that my so-called traumas—the death of the daughter, the abuse in my childhood, the rage I carried and acted out as a teen and young adult—were places of storytelling. Realms of expression.

Thirty years later the quality of my sadness has changed so radically that I can only understand it as pure creativity. In every book I have ever written there is a girl. And there always will be. Beyond forever, since I no longer believe in linear time. Into star stuff.

My daughter's name was Lily.

My grief and my daughter's death and my suffering were not something to "get over" or medicate or counsel out of me. They were *generative* of the most important forms of self-expression I'll ever create in my lifetime. And that doesn't just matter for my career as a writer, or even for my mental and emotional health as a woman. It's also the path I took to learn love, so that when my son came, sun of my life, I was able to give it with abandon and joy.

Death, grief, trauma are alive in our actual bodies. We carry them our whole lives, even if we act like it's possible to "step out of them." Writing, making stories, drawing and painting and making art doesn't release me from loss or grief or trauma, but it does let me re-story my self and my body. In this sense, to be a misfit means to be willing to dive into the waters of one's life, swim to the wreckage at the bottom, and bring something back to the surface. We have to find the forms of expression that will let us *move* the story.

When I tell you that literature and writing have saved my life, perhaps you can believe me when I say they came into my body and lodged in the space that my daughter left open. If you are one of those people who has the ability to make it down to the bottom of the ocean, the ability to swim the dark waters without fear, the astonishing ability to move through life's worst crucibles and not die, then you also have the ability to bring something back to the surface that helps others in a way that they cannot achieve themselves.

You are not nothing.

You are vital to your culture.

We misfits are the ones with the ability to enter grief. Death. Trauma. And emerge. But we have to keep telling our stories, giving them to each other, or they will eat us alive. Our suffering is not the Christ story. Our suffering is generative of secular meaning. We put ordinary forms of hope into the world so that others, scruffy or graceful, might go on.

•   •   •

I first met my friend Jordan Foster through a mutual friend of ours, the national best-selling thriller author Chelsea Cain. Chelsea Cain has a big personality. She is brilliant and funny and beautiful and socially wonderful. The truth is, sometimes Jordan and I huddle together in a corner, or a bedroom, or near the exits at Chelsea's fantastic parties, because, well, misfits try to go to their friends' parties even though we know we are terrible at it. I once spent an hour in her laundry room trying to regain my composure. Never underestimate the comforting smell of small, miraculous dryer sheets. What Jordan and I have in common is an inability to fit in comfortably.

Anywhere.

And so we have developed a bond, one that is also woven through with our love for writing and animals, especially not-quite-right animals like hairless ones. I identify with Jordan's experiences of glancing off various ocean bottoms as well as her description of misfittery.

Missing the fit . . . I am different, I am other. Perhaps there is, at some points in life, a sense of pride in not belonging, or in belonging in a different way. But for the most part, there is only a sense of distance between yourself and the sea of other people who fit, who belong, who move fluidly when you are a body of waves—tidal and sneaker and everything in between that push and pull you to places that aren't quite in tune with the rest of the world. The thing about being a misfit for me—and I can't and don't want to speak for anyone else—is the fact that it's a known quantity, a part of me that, though it cannot be hidden, can be pummeled and reshaped into something resembling normalcy. I can paint a convincing picture of fitting, minus the "mis-," if the situation calls for it. But I never identify with the person I become in the moments when I fit and blend. It's fake. I'm fake. I know I don't fit.

Everyone is a misfit in the way that everyone is human. It's a sweeping generalization that belittles the fact that there are people who truly feel that they do not belong. (This is a wholly separate idea, though there are undeniably elements of crossover, between those who feel like they don't fit in the bodies they were born into, or to the gender or sexual identity that society wants to ascribe to them to make categorization easier. That deep sense of belonging to something other than what you are given is the fodder for another essay.) But the idea that we're all misfits so why don't we all get along is, honestly, bullshit. If we were all misfits, it would mean we all fit. We don't. And that matters. Being a misfit doesn't make you inhuman any more than fitting in makes you human. There is a spectrum for all things. Some of us are on the far side of fitting in, even when we're using a spectrum of our making. And when we try and measure ourselves using the values set forth by a group of people who don't understand that life is loud and overwhelming and oftentimes feels like a torrent of dirty water rising up, inexorable and lung-stoppingily cold, from the bottom of a well whose slippery walls you're only barely clinging to? We don't even register on that scale.

The older I get, the more my choices dictate the degree to which I fit into the world, the amount I allow my misfit identity to bleed through. I denied it for a long time, which was ridiculous, like denying the fact that I needed glasses or would never be tall enough to play basketball in anything better than a mediocre rec league. I don't fit, I'd tell myself, because I'm not trying hard enough. I threw myself into school, always. It became the space where I could if not fit, at least excel. And if I stood out, it was because of achievement, not difference. The gap that appeared between my peers and myself—and I make no claims to any genius on my part—only made me more convinced, paradoxically, that I did not fit. I did not fit with the "smart kids." I did not fit with the slackers. The only person I truly fit with was myself, and my brain laid waste to that idea, doing a fine job during my school career—all the way through graduate school—convincing me that there was nowhere I truly belonged but, it chided, by the way, I was still not achieving my full potential.

It's a strange thing, being a misfit in your own mind, the place that can also be a refuge. For most of my life, I've cherished nothing more than being alone, because being alone if you don't fit is like being in a place where you make the fewest mistakes, you know the fewest people with whom to make awkward conversation, and you're generally the safest. And yet recently, I've cautiously welcomed the occasional interloper. The mind is a dangerous place when you're certain you don't belong on the outside and you're not entirely certain you belong on the inside, either. Sometimes outside reason can be essential. Not all the time and not as any kind of cure (being a misfit is far from an affliction that needs fixing), but as a candle handed over when the lights are out for too long.

If I knew what would help I'd do it more often. We'd all do it more often. Easy, and fake, answers to this question are the kind you find on the Internet at 3 AM when you're googling things that are too complex to google yet you do it anyway: How do I live with how I am when it's not in step with how the world works? How can I be in a world when I don't know how to be in my own? These are not questions that yield millions of (useful) hits. I'd like to say that I write and that makes it better. Sometimes it does. Sometimes it feels more like I borrowed a spotlight and spray paint and high-lighted my failures, in case I didn't already know them by heart, in my heart, as if they did not beat into me as my heart beats. But sometimes putting the not-fitting into words and sentences and paragraphs that do fit because grammar fits can soothe the roiling and put up a levy, at least temporarily, to the torrent inside. Yet levies break. They always do. That's why there is no permanent solution, no way to force fitting when you don't. You can walk in the silence of an early morning or the muted bustle of the city late at night, and for a few minutes or an hour, you'll be in a rhythm and you'll think, This, this is how it can be. But it's not like that. The key is to find enough of those moments of rhythm so that the in-between lulls don't pull you down and out and under, into a place where it doesn't matter if you fit or don't fit. Even if you don't fit, you must always care.

If we tell our children anything, it must be that fitting in is not what's important. It's what's easy. It's what's expected and so the opposite is frowned upon. We should tell them that it hurts not to belong and, as hard as it might be to hear, that hurt may not go away. It may grow and settle into a different, deeper kind of hurt, a pain that seeps and spreads and becomes a part of them. It's not sadness, exactly. Misfits can, and often are, happy, joyful, blissful people. But for some, there was a shift at some point, at the cartilage level, when the realization of difference took hold. Some people embrace this. Others store it away, using it as a secret greeting, a handshake between like-minded individuals at a party no one quite wanted to attend. For children who don't fit, the worst thing we can do is tell them to try harder to change and be like the ones who do. There is power in difference. There is beauty.

4 Standing Up Inside Your Dream

When I first met my dream, I was a messed-up, malcontent, miserable misfit. I couldn't have been more NOT READY to meet my dream. Up until that moment, all I was was a survivor. I'd survived my father's abuse, two divorces, flunking out of college, addiction, rehab, and incarceration. And, as noted, I'd lost most of my marbles when my daughter died, and I'd spent some time living under an overpass in the great altered state of mega grief and loss. So what I'm saying is, when I met my dream, my misfit status nearly killed it.

Luckily, not all dreams come from looking up. If you're a messed-up, malcontent, miserable misfit, and you are still alive, dreams can sometimes appear out of nowhere—so if you are out there, remember I said this: Sometimes there's a dream underneath the dream, or to the side of it, or cutting right through it.

It started so small. In my hands. In the winter of my early thirties, I sent a short story out to a writing contest. The short story was called "The Chronology of Water." It was a story about how my daughter's death nearly killed me. About how I saved my father's life when he almost drowned, even though he was our abuser. I sent the story four places: to the admissions committee for the MFA in writing at Columbia University; to the hiring committee for a tenure-track teaching position in writing at San Diego State University; to Literary Arts in Oregon as a writing sample for a grant; and to *Poets & Writers* as a writing sample for the Maureen Egen Writers Exchange Award.

In the spring, in the space of a month, my mailbox presented me with four letters—white and geometric and smelling of something like "what if."

I was accepted to Columbia University to pursue an MFA.

I was offered a tenure-track teaching job.

I was awarded a $3,000 grant for my writing.

And I won the *Poets & Writers* Exchange Award, which meant a trip to New York City to meet with famous editors, agents, and writers.

When I looked at the four letters on my kitchen table I did what all people like me do. I poured a giant tumbler of vodka, with lime and ice, and stared at them for an entire day, afraid to move. I think I was waiting to see if the letters would float to the floor like the rest of my dreams had.

Eventually, me being me, I chose the job offer over the MFA. This is important—the MFA was what I wanted more than anything. You have no idea. With all my broken little heart. It was the only big dream I'd ever had in my life—to become a writer! But I couldn't choose it. I had to survive. I had to take care of myself. No one else would. And so I swallowed the desire to name myself as a writer who would go to Columbia. Prestige was not my name. Get a job was my name. Suck it up and move forward was my name. Misfits and screwups don't become successful writers.

Similarly, I took the grant money and bought a car. I'd already been stealing one steak a week from Safeway to get some protein in my body, so when I saw money, my survival instincts won out. Oh, I wanted to go to Paris, fill my bathtub with champagne, and buy ten pairs of Dr. Martens in ten different colors as well as a black leather biker jacket, but I bought a car instead. A reliable car to get to and from work. A used Toyota pickup. I didn't take myself out to dinner, I didn't buy myself champagne, I didn't eat chocolate. I didn't even tell anyone.

Thank God the "go to New York Writers Exchange Award" didn't have a practical alternative for self-destructive dreamless people or I would have let that go, too. Almost in spite of myself then, I went to New York. You know, where the writers are. Where the dream lives.

The "prize" of winning a Writers Exchange Award from *Poets & Writers* is that you go from one state to another—in my case, Oregon to New York. You get to choose the writers you'd most like to meet while you are there, and the *Poets & Writers* folks try very hard to arrange meetings. You get to give a reading at a *very* fancy poetry center, you get to stay at the Gramercy Park Hotel and drink scotch into the night with swank, smart, cool people as if you are one too, you get to meet editors and publishers and writers and agents at very fancy lunches and dinners. How fancy? I kept three of the linen napkins. I also stole a menu from one restaurant. I still have these keepsakes. From 1996.

The four writers I selected to meet were Carole Maso, Peggy Phelan, Lynne Tillman, and Eurydice. I know! Likely many of you have never heard of them. But what I'm telling you is, to me, these four women were TITANS. And besides, these women lit my brain on fire.

In New York, four of the most humbling and happy nights of my entire life happened to me. Dinners that lasted for hours and cost more than my rent and car payments. Food that tasted so good I thought I might faint—I mean I'd hold each bite in my mouth so long it would dissolve. Wine that didn't turn your teeth purple, it actually made your teeth melt in your mouth. And the women! These now over fifty-year-old women writers were so intelligent, so creative, so gorgeous and present in their own minds and bodies . . . I mean I nearly barfed, peed, and orgasmed all at the same time. Screw heaven. Screw Paris. Screw chocolate and Dr. Martens. These women were alive in their minds. Maybe it sounds weird but I'd never experienced that before.

Their writing was intentionally unconventional. Wild. Passionate. Blood-bodied, unapologetic. And all four insisted on the body as content in their stories. They were not main-stream writers. They were not best sellers. They were carving out astonishing paths of their own quite to the side of main-stream, maybe in spite of it, maybe the way water cut the Grand Canyon. I wanted my writing to go like theirs. Follow it. I felt like their writing had parted the seas for people like me.

I can't tell you how many times I choked up talking to each of these women. Looking into their eyes. Trying to feel a self I could make from their words. I don't think I said much of anything at all. It's possible I went mute. It's hard to remember anything about myself. Though I remember nearly every word each of them said. Of this I am sure: I was never as . . . creatively happy. This strange "prize" of sitting with four intellectual, creative, not-sorry women writers. A rare thing.

What an opportunity, huh? Oregon writer hits the big-time. New York City! No bigger dream for a wannabe writer. Still makes me smile remembering it, all these years later.

But there is a bittersweetness in my throat, too. A small stone I carry there. The small stone of sad that came from my inability to be the writer that my dream required—the dream where you hit it big in New York City. I was on a journey all right, but this isn't a hero story.

I was taken to meet an editor at Farrar, Straus and Giroux. He talked to me about my life as a swimmer, and he suggested I had a book in me about my swimmer's life. I don't know, say, like a memoir. I stood there like a numb idiot smiling and shaking my head with my arms crossed over my chest. He waited for me to jump at his suggestion. But you know what? Nothing nothing nothing came out of my throat. He shook my hand and wished me luck. He patted my shoulder like a swim coach might. He gave me some free books.

Later, I sat at dinner between Lynn Tillman and the world-renowned, beloved W. W. Norton editor Carol Houck Smith—who sadly has since died—while Lynne tried to persuade Carol to publish me at Norton. Carol Houck Smith, who leaned over and said, "Well, then send me something." Her bright, fierce little eyes staring right through my know-nothing skull.

Most people would have stepped off the plane back in Oregon and RUN to the post office. But a misfit? It took me over a decade to even imagine putting something in an envelope and sealing it.

After the reading at the fancy poetry center, a big-time literary agent came up to me and asked if I'd like representation. On the spot. My small sad throat stone. I went deaf and smiled and shook her hand. I thought I might cry in front of all the dressed-up people. All that came out of my mouth was "I don't know."

She said, "Okay then."

All those open hands held out to me.

I'm trying to tell you something important. About people like me. About misfits. You see, it is important to understand how damaged people don't always know how to say yes, or to choose the big thing, even when it is right in front of them. It's a shame we carry. The shame of wanting something good. The shame of feeling something good. The shame of not believing we deserve to stand in the same big room in the same way as all those we admire.

If I could go back, I'd coach myself. I'd be exactly like those women I met. I'd be the fearless, intelligent, creative woman who taught me how to stand up, how to want things, how to ask for them. I'd be the over-fifty woman who says, *Your mind, your imagination, they are everything. Look how beautiful. Yes, you. You deserve to sit at the table. The radiance falls on all of us. We're nothing without all of us.*

I knew even on the plane back west as the evergreens and rivers of Oregon came into view through the perfect drizzle of home that if I was a woman writer at all, then I was a damaged kind of woman writer. I drank many tiny bottles of airplane feel-sorry-for-yourself. What I'm saying is that I flew back to Oregon without a book deal, without an agent, with only a head and heart full of beautiful memories about what it would be like to be a well-known writer, since I'd sat so near them, since I'd eaten with them and shared such perfect company. It was the only prize I allowed myself.

And yet alone, at home, in the quiet, I could still hear them. Those women writers. They said: "Don't listen to anyone who tells you to change your voice. Find your voice and never look back" and "Sometimes telling the story IS saving your own life."

Now I'm the woman over fifty. A mother. A teacher. A woman writer. Although it didn't happen when that dream letter arrived in my mailbox, the first memoir I published is called *The Chronology of Water.* In it I tell the story of how many times I've had to reinvent a self. How many times my seeming failures were really just weird portals to something beautiful. All I had to do was recognize the writer already inside me and listen.

You can be a drunk. You can be a survivor of abuse. You can be an ex-con. You can be a homeless person. You can lose all your money or your job or a husband or a wife, or the worst thing imaginable, a child. You can lose your marbles. You can be standing inside your own failure, a small sad stone in your throat, and still you are beautiful, your story is worth hearing, because you—you rare and phenomenal misfit—are the only one in the world who can tell the story the way that only you can.

I'll be listening.

●   ●   ●

When I met my friend Althea Heustis Wollf, she was a graduate student in the low-residency MFA program at Eastern

Oregon University, one of the many places that I am lucky enough to teach.

Althea did not make eye contact with me for three days. The things she said in class were a little like jagged agitator particles in the room. The questions she raised made people uncomfortable.

I loved her instantly.

Althea's journey as a writer means stepping in and out of cultural stories. I believe she is a new species—and by that I mean we have a new generation of writers and artists coming who have emerged in spite of all of our cultural divisions like first teeth cutting through flesh. This is her story:

As a girl there already is a scale of conformity we have to measure up to in society. Girls have to carry unfair standards in American society, which continues to change, especially with the latest election results. As a Native American who is also white, the balance of that scale was and continues to be modified. My initial response to this kind of judgment, access to opportunity or to having your voice heard, is anger and protest. I have tried, most of the time, to utilize processes, hoping because of who I am or what I am that my voice will not be muffled or overlooked.

I am a misfit. I am a woman. I speak up. I know my laws and how to amend them, and because I am calm and focused in my delivery, stating facts, I am a threat to closed minds. It's time for change— it's overdue. I'm a misfit.

I was brought up in a colorful culture that revolved around the environment; everything from hunting, gathering, our religion in the sweathouse to living so far out in the country. Fun was roaming around the hills and riding horses. Early in my childhood we saw changes in the river: cows having to go farther up to drink from springs while out gathering, not swimming in the creeks. This upbringing caused me to think in a different way from my peers. There were layers of anger or guilt these people had, because I'm a girl speaking up, [because] I'm a Native American, and because I spoke out against how people treated girls/women and the environment—a concept not popular in rural America. My own white aunt told me I was brainwashed by my Native culture and that what happened to us was progress. Get over it.

Having a new culture of misfits gives me some confidence that I will not be the only one influencing change in the way ALL people view the environment, that America is Native land and we're still here, and of course, valuing women by ensuring they will continue to have human rights.

I didn't know my family was raising me to be this way. I honestly thought I was wrong most of the time, but they have my back and now I have an even bigger family—my fellow misfit writer family—because of the way they raised me. The saying in my family is: Raise the children to be Bears. Bears are seen as leaders. They live separate lives, living within the laws of the Creator, but always keeping one another in check. Bears usually don't worry about what another Bear has; they live their own lives. When it comes to times of celebration and even tension, we come together just like Bears.

Understanding being a misfit helped me have confidence that there are more people out there like me. I do not have to be so stressed out. There are brilliant people out there who want Native

Americans around, who want a clean environment and human rights for women. It is a comfort in these trying times. Someday we can lay to rest the title of Misfit, memorialize it. I have faith in these artists and writers that are fighting for generations they will never see, just as I am doing.

I find myself feeling like a misfit in a circle of misfits. Then I remember how much horseshit that way of thinking is, because we need each other. In a survey given to my community at an event, people were asked if they would listen to someone who survived addiction more than someone who found a way to avoid becoming an addict. The responses were exactly half and half. Comments included that people would rather hear from someone who's been there. It was the elderly and the young who wanted to know how someone could prevent addiction. So I say misfits in the area of addiction are very much needed, and I would add that this is true for all topics related to being a misfit. People need our stories. Our stories are a form of knowledge.

5 The Misfit as Artist

I suppose this anthem will soon age out, but for a lot of us who are adults right now, the Island of Misfit Toys scene in the television holiday special *Rudolph the Red-Nosed Reindeer* is kind of a theme song, theme story, life theme. Oh how we loved the Charlie-in-the-Box, the spotted elephant, a bird that swims, a cowboy that rides an ostrich, a train with square wheels on its caboose, a water pistol that shoots jelly, a grounded plane, and a scooter with two wheels in front and one in back. Here's some fun trivia that matters to us, too: Dolly was a seemingly normal girl rag doll. Her misfit problem is never explained on the special; many years later, on NPR's *Wait Wait . . . Don't Tell Me!* news quiz show (broadcast December 8, 2007), *Rudolph's* producer, Arthur Rankin Jr., noted that Dolly's problem was *psychological*, caused by being abandoned by her owner and leading her to suffer from depression.[3]

In fact, Rudolph, Yukon Cornelius, and the Bumble (the Abominable Snow Monster) also qualify as a posse we can identify with.

How important is it for kids to have images like the Misfit Toys, Edward Scissorhands, Napoleon Dynamite, or characters like those in *The Goonies*, *Scott Pilgrim vs. the World*, or *Diary of a Wimpy Kid* in their lives? I think some of us might say lifesaving. That's how important.

In my own life, in addition to Rudolph, what else helped was Charlie Brown. *Harold and Maude. Cool Hand Luke. Annie Hall. Carrie. One Flew Over the Cuckoo's Nest. The Breakfast Club. The Crow.* And anything by Tim Burton or Wes Anderson, forever.

What I'm getting at is, partly how misfits get through life without exiting is that we occasionally see representations of ourselves that help. We see that the character who mis-fits or is outcast has their own kind of weird beauty or meaning, even if it is not always the same as the hero's happy ending. Napoleon Dynamite and Edward Scissorhands, for instance, do not get to lead any sleigh ride. But they do earn the right to a place in the world that is utterly original. Randle P. McMurphy is lobotomized and neutralized forever, but his spirit is reborn inside Chief Bromden forever. Carrie doesn't live, but her ghost does, and reminds us how ugly we are when we commit the sin of othering anyone who is different from the conforming masses and their rituals of beauty and popularity.

The first time I watched *Napoleon Dynamite* I got a stomachache. I didn't laugh once. It felt too real, the scenes too close to home. His weirdness was too accurate. I almost couldn't watch it.

Every single subsequent viewing I got stronger. Now it is one of my favorite movies, because I can laugh, I can bring a little distance to the images; I've experienced a kind of healing through the art that I did not experience as a teen in life. In a very real sense, that movie helped me go back and mend a small segment of my development that never happened, because I got stuck there. My home life in my teens was claustrophobic, abusive, a horror. Simultaneously, I was not fitting into any group or clique at school. My only safety was aloneness. So it felt like there was nowhere to exist—not at home, not at school. Watching or reading a character go through that kind of isolation from weirdness or difference to, if not social integration, then at least a moment of social meaning, can literally put our souls back together. I can watch the character now and love him, cheer for him, glory in his last weird dance exactly like the audience does in the movie when they stand and clap. I still own a pair of the original moon boots. Sometimes I wear them to feel privately fantastic.

I used to watch the films *One Flew Over the Cuckoo's Nest* and *To Kill A Mockingbird* on my birthday. They were, for a long while in my twenties, my favorite movies and books. In both, the misfits have moments of glory—like when Boo Radley saves both Scout and Scout's brother, Jem, how he leaves treasures in a tree for children to find. Or when Randle takes the "nuts" out boating and fishing by persuading them to pose as doctors. Or when Chief reveals that he is neither deaf nor mute, and smiles wider than an Oregon river. Or when Chief throws that goddamn sink thing straight out the window and leaves the mental health ward that is murdering their souls forever.

I saw *One Flew Over the Cuckoo's Nest* seven times and read the novel three times before I ever met the author, Ken Kesey. How I came to meet him was that I infiltrated a creative writing class at the University of Oregon. I was a returning undergraduate at the time, having flunked out in Texas. My friend Meredith was a graduate student in the MFA program. When Ken Kesey agreed to teach a yearlong fiction writing class, Meredith smuggled me in. So my first big-time writing class was basically a combined act of infiltration and accident.

You could say that Ken Kesey was the epitome of a misfit, if misfits aspire toward such a thing. And we do. Everything he ever wrote and every moment of his life resisted conforming to anything else around him. To be entirely honest with you, if I had not met him when I did, a year after the death of my daughter, shortly after I discovered weird writing coming out of me from nowhere, I might have missed the profoundly important portal that opened up right in front of me that brought me to my life as a writer. In several ways that count, he was much more important to me than my father.

And if he had not whispered into my ear the words that he did the first time I met him, "I know what happened to you. Death's a motherfucker," bonding us in a single second with two dead children between us, my beautiful tiny girl infant and his beautifully strong wrestler son, second selves, hovering between our bodies, I don't know if I would have trusted anyone or anything in the world again.

Sometimes a single sentence whispered from the mouth of a misfit can change your life.

I've written about what it was like to walk into a room and meet Ken Kesey for the first time. I've written about the yearlong novel writing class, how we lived in a rented house off and on near campus with Kesey, how we visited his farm in Pleasant Hill, how we came to understand various other misfit characters like Wavy Gravy and Garrison Keillor and Tim Leary and Tom

Wolfe and Hunter S. Thompson and the strange wonder that was Neal Cassady, whose ghost image we only saw in home movies.

I wondered where and how the women fit into the story. Or maybe I longed for it, long for it still.

Kesey went to the University of Oregon, the main reason I chose that college. He graduated in 1957, and after that he had a fellowship at Stanford, where he wrote *Cuckoo's Nest*. The inspiration for the novel came from his work on the night shift at Menlo Park Veterans Hospital. Because Kesey was Kesey, he'd get high on hallucinogens and talk to the patients there. He told us much later in life in that yearlong class we took with him that he did not believe the patients were insane, but rather that society had outcast them because they did not fit the conventional ideas of how people were supposed to act and behave. Maybe knowing Kesey is how I came to understand the possibility that being a misfit isn't nothing.

That it might, in fact, be everything.

After Kesey moved to La Honda, California, he began hosting hippie artist happenings and became part of the Merry Pranksters; he was a proponent of marijuana and LSD. In 1965, Kesey was arrested for marijuana possession as well as a faked suicide, and he spent about six months in jail.

In 2014, marijuana was legalized in Oregon. Today, the pot business is thriving. I can't help but wonder about that. One year you can be arrested and put in jail for something that years later will become legal.

Truths change. Stories are what happen between truth's ever-changing incarnations. Misfits tell the best stories because our very lives depend on navigating an ever-changing reality.

Quite often, misfits turn into artists of one sort or another. Making art is the most intense form of expression available to humans, and it is a real place where a misfit can not only exist, but also find community without judgment. Artists are very good at stepping into and owning their misfit natures, because we *want* to live at the edges of culture, since the center didn't make any sense to us and made us feel ugly or fat or stupid or crazy or weird or deviant or unwelcome. Art is a kind of cultural medicine. Sometimes, for example, when you give juvenile offenders a canvas or a blank page or a musical instrument and let them access self-expression, their self-destruction begins to change and even fall away. Not always, but sometimes.

Sometimes misfit artists turn into misfit addicts. Kesey was and wasn't an addict. That's not an easy sentence to understand the way we see things today, but it's true.

What I haven't written about is just how much I miss him. It hurts that he is gone. It's as if he took something with him that he was in the middle of handing to me, to us, and then he died, leaving us reaching. Maybe that's a good thing—that he left us reaching. Maybe the fact that he showed us that we were not alone, that we could walk into a room and for once feel that, mercifully, there were others, and that his death kept us reaching . . . Maybe that's a kind of misfit inspiration. But I find his spirit in so many others.

●   ●   ●

I first met my brilliant and beautiful friend Melissa Febos on the page when I read her memoir *Whip Smart*, in which she describes the four years she worked as a dominatrix in a Midtown dungeon. She described that part of her life as a "hell of her own making," an idea I could relate to, as well as her experiences as a high school dropout and her drug and alcohol use. Let me tell you, her story is one of the most bold and clear expressions of the human condition I have ever clapped eyes on. Later in life when I met her in person, I do not think it would be an exaggeration to say that our body stories made a helix of sorts. In some ways I think of her as a sister, certainly of the body and soul, even as our lives are not the same. I feel like our life story evolutions carry pieces of each other. Here is her story about being a misfit artist.

I do think that the experience of being a misfit in the respect that you name—being an outsider up against social norms—was a problem in my own experience that found a solution in art-making. By "problem," I mean in the sense that Chekhov meant when he said "the task of the writer is not to solve the problem but to state the problem correctly." Which is to say, being a misfit and incapable of conforming to social norms was painful, it was incontrovertible, and it forced me to find my truest calling, which has been so profound and that I would not trade for any better kind of fit. I was a strange and secretive child who buried things in the backyard, was aware of my queerness very young, and read books with the same voracity that I later shot heroin. My mother was a bisexual, feminist, Buddhist psychotherapist who raised me vegetarian and corrected the sexism of my children's books with a Sharpie, and my father was a Puerto Rican sea captain. I say all this to make the point that there was no getting around it: I was different; we were different.

Those differences led me to a lot of dark places, and by "dark" I mean not illuminated by cultural reference and acknowledgment, or curtained by stigma. For instance, my discomfort with the power dynamics I experienced, particularly as a woman, coupled with my interest in chasing down my own sexual curiosity and hunger, led me to answering an ad in the Village Voice *when I was twenty-one. There was no mirror in the world of television and school and magazines for the kind of female I was, the kind of feminine. For models of tenderness and catharsis that included violence. So I showed up at this secret place in Midtown Manhattan, and there I created a persona, a character of myself whom I called by a different name—Justine—through whom I could embody and enact these parts of me that seemed misfit in the brighter world outside those rooms. I remember once relating to this client of mine, a Hasidic man thirty years my senior, who described the shame and loneliness inherent in his secret life, in which he frequented our "dungeon." Similarly, I found identification among the junkies with whom I copped and used in my late teens and early twenties— we had all ended up in seemingly corrupt places out of a desire to solve or comfort or find company in our misfit parts. And in many ways, those places met our need.*

I have found that I can even better meet that need with art and other artists. I can go to all the dark places (without risking my life) and find companions as a result of sharing my journeys. And all the aspects of my strangeness and my family's strangeness—our misfittedness—have factored into the art I make in a very transparent way. All my work tells secrets, and I use the vocabulary I gleaned from my origins—psychotherapy textbooks, the texts I read over and over, and the catalog of images that filled my childhood. I suspect that there are writers who didn't come to writing as a method of survival, of carving a space in the world that they would fit in, but I don't actually know any writers like that. My friends and peers are a pretty self-selecting group, and we found each other precisely because of our common misfittedness; those odd angles are the things we most share and love in each other.

To me, art is that most profound form of expression because it integrates the body, experience, intellect, and the senses. It is the most holistic and therefore the most precise way of articulating our humanity. In it, we can see most quickly how alike we are, how not alone. In the most general terms, I would define it that way.

For me, personally, it is that and more. My nature is one of avoidance and dissociation, one of constant motion. I'm compulsive, addictive, pleasure-seeking, conflict avoidant, and all these inherent qualities would have killed me, quite literally, if not for writing. The momentum of my appetites—as when I was an active drug addict, a sex worker, and in bondage to an excoriating and relentless love affair—is not an easy thing to arrest, let alone reverse. The only thing that can do it is intense self-scrutiny coupled with the love and witness of other people, and possibly also, God (whatever that may mean). Carl Jung described addiction as a low-level spiritual quest, and suggested that the only cure is a spiritual awakening, and connection with other people.

Once, when I was in the midst of that relentless love affair, I called my mother. I was crying every single day, completely

obsessed with my lover and trying to wrest from her some kind
of security that was simply more than any single human can give
another, and the rest of my life was basically in shambles. I didn't
confide in many people, because I found my messiness and my
need so repulsive and humiliating. But this one day I just called my
mom. "I'm a wreck," I told her. "I can't stop crying." And she told
me this story about how I had been a colicky baby, and how as an
older child I simply stopped crying. My dad would be leaving for sea
voyages, a thing that had always been very painful, and one day I
just stopped crying completely. In that short exchange, something
important happened. First, I exposed my supposed brokenness to
someone else. Secondly, as a result, I was offered some context for it.
That little bit of information somehow "normalized" my wrecked
state, made a kind of sense of it. And it was right after that that I
decided to write about it.

That is, I think all my "self-destructive" impulses are misguided
attempts at connection, at looking for a higher power in unqual-
ified places. And writing is my solution. In it, I am able to look
at myself, and I am able to expose myself to other people. In that
vulnerable place I become capable of both giving and receiving love.
I find something more qualified in which to thrust my faith, something that can hold all of it, all of me.

So, I think "artistic practice" is survival. It is community. It is
forgiveness. It is my religion and my god, or my channel to God.

I think "regular people" can learn how to acknowledge their
own misfit parts by watching us do it. When I published my first
book, in which I describe smoking crack and spanking strangers
and feeling like the only woman in the world with so many secrets,

I was shocked to discover how many strangers, how many "regular people," identified with my experience. They hadn't smoked crack or been sex workers, but they had felt howlingly alone inside their own experiences. My story, of accepting my dark parts, and the airing of that story, gave them license to hope the same might be possible for them.

Performing this inhabitation of self is a great service, I think. It is the most beautiful kind of martyrdom, in which you sacrifice your own comfort (temporarily), your own secrecy, your own shabby means of fake fitting-in, for the benefit of witnesses, of "regular people" (or, as I like to call them, "civilians"). But, instead of dying, you get to be free. And they get to see that it is possible.

Instead of dying, we get to be free. I love that idea so very much. In some ways I think that all artists are misfits, and what I see when I think about that is that we are the edges of a shape that contains everyone else. We are the edges that define whether or not the center will hold and what shape will eventually emerge. I think art is the most profound form of human expression available. We keep culture breathing.

6 The Misfit as Addict

There's a short story that I love beyond measure, one that made all the hairs on my arms and legs stand up when I first read it; I may have held my breath reading the last page, I may or may not have burst into tears. One I have taught in nearly every classroom I've entered for the last twenty-eight years. It's called "Sonny's Blues" by James Baldwin. One of the many reasons I love this story is that it is about a bona fide misfit, Sonny, who the narrator of the story, his brother, is struggling to understand. Sonny is a heroin and alcohol addict. He is also a brilliant jazz pianist.

The story opens with the narrator, who teaches at a school in Harlem filled with boys who remind him of his brother—boys with not much of a future ahead of them. The narrator is also trying to process the news that his younger brother has been arrested in a heroin bust.

While the narrator goes off to war, his mother dies. His mother made him promise to look after Sonny. The narrator tries to talk to Sonny after the funeral, trying to understand his brother's choices. When he asks Sonny what he wants to do with his life, Sonny says he wants to be a jazz musician. The narrator does not in any way understand this decision and even throws shade on Sonny's dream. The two of them try to figure out how to move forward, where Sonny might live and what he should do with his life; they do not agree on those topics and argue.

Eventually the brothers come to an agreement. If Sonny stays in school, he can play the piano in Isabel's parent's house whenever he wants.

Sonny doesn't keep going to school. He does what his passion is. He goes to Greenwich Village to be with his jazz friends. He does drugs. So Sonny leaves the house, drops out of school, and joins the navy.

The brothers both return from war and end up living in New York City. Sometimes they see each other. When they do, they fight. But when the narrator's daughter Gracie dies, he decides he wants to be in touch with Sonny—something about suffering creates the urge in him to reconnect: "My trouble made his real."

As adults then, Sonny invites the narrator to come hear him play in Greenwich Village. For the first time, Sonny talks to his brother about his heroin addiction, what it feels like in his veins. Sonny says it makes you feel in control, and sometimes you just have to feel that way, because the rest of life makes you feel out of control. They discuss how many ways there are to suffer. None of them are beautiful, but they are real.

At the jazz club, the narrator realizes how talented and respected Sonny is there. He listens to Sonny play, and soon the entire room is mesmerized by the quality of his performance. When the narrator experiences the passion of Sonny's music, he decides to send him a cup of milk and scotch, there at the piano, where his brother is his best self.

The reason this story got so deeply under my skin is that I

read it as a misfit story. I identify with Sonny even as I realize we are not the same. I understand how different our experiences are, and why, and yet I am a person who can sit in a room with another so-called junkie or addict and listen to their story without judgment. I feel a strange kind of kindred. They could be me. Or you.

I'll say it bald: I'm your garden-variety functional addict with the annoying ability to kick. My clean and sober brothers and sisters are rolling their eyes right now. And maybe they're right. Maybe there is no such place. There's nothing special about my status. I'm everywhere, in between all the people we like to outcast, on the one hand, when we demonize back-alley junkies or people who break the law or poor people, and the safer, whiter, bourgeois version which I have settled into over time and age, that is, the seemingly well-adjusted, income-earning parent, spouse, so-called good citizen. I'm both, because in a particularly privileged way, I feel compelled to add, since unlike most people of color, I received second chances when I made terrible mistakes.

Let me get a couple of things straight from the get-go. Clean, dependent, and addicted are three different categories. All three retain a relationship to addiction. Secondly, traditionally in this country, and up until quite recently, addicts have been outcast and punished like criminals. So I'm going to tell you my story, but I want you to understand that the position from which I am speaking is privileged. Mine is not the most important story to listen to. But maybe my story can contribute to those that help people learn to listen differently.

Heroin made me feel like I didn't have to live with the life and body I was given. Like alcohol, it gave me respite and a kind of freedom unavailable to me without it. At the time, in my twenties, I would have gone anywhere and done anything to have a life not mine.

Read that sentence again. It's a death drive sentence. It's important.

When I kicked heroin the first time I did it locked in a one-room apartment with two people who agreed to take turns watching over me, washing my sheets and body while the sweat and toxins exuded until the poison was out. It took nineteen days, give or take the rest of your life. Nineteen days that felt like having seven kinds of flu for a year. It's brutal, kicking, even if you are one of the lucky ones. And by "lucky" I mean "able to kick," since I profoundly understand how it might not seem possible no matter how much help is available, and for the record, not much help is available yet. I was fairly certain several different times that I had died. The nightmares, lucid dreams, and hallucinations I had rivaled Hieronymus Bosch's paintings of hell.

Or war zones, which legions of people—including children—live and die in without much choice.

In terms of addiction, the danger zone for someone like me at this point isn't necessarily any one particular substance, although I've personally had the hardest time with heroin, alcohol, and Vicodin at different times in my life. The danger zone for people like me is that I'll lock on to almost anything else as I'm depriving myself of the "dangerous" thing. It's hilarious in a lot of ways. My son has to continuously steer me away from Diet Pepsi at the grocery store. If you are not already aware of this, soda is made of poison. But even if you think Diet Pepsi is safe and sound, the problem for me isn't so much the Diet Pepsi. It's that when I lock on to something addictively, as a habit of mind, a structure of consciousness, a physical drive, it is possible I can't stop myself. I mean if he isn't with me, I'll make a beeline. If he's there, he just has to gently guide me by the elbow and maneuver the cart toward bread or milk.

Another kind of misfit, then, is the addict. The recovering addict as well as the addict in the throes of their addiction. I truly wish we had better words for all that though, because increasingly the gap between the so-called addicted person and the so-called not addicted person is closing.

Addiction may be the logical extension of late capitalism.

Here is something important to think through: whereas some misfits are identifiable to us because they live at the edges of culture, like rebellious artists, or homeless people, or institutionalized people, the addict misfit can hide in plain sight.

Maybe we are not so different, misfits and others. Maybe even well-adjusted people run to 5 PM for their wine-on. Maybe we all feel a little bit more frenzied desire than is normal buying the next iPhone. Facebook is a place I can spend entire days and nights . . . maybe that's all of us. And how many of us have spent too long obsessively exploring WebMD? And how good are any of us at not eating the entire bag of potato chips or the entire bar of sea salt and caramel chocolate or drinking pickle juice from the jar at 2 AM?

What's not as funny is the way I used relationships or sexuality or self-destruction or self-sabotage in my past as surrogates for "high" or "drunk." Anything to fill the hole in us that keeps us from feeling whole. Anything to push the dopamine around in my body.

What I'm saying is, the addiction gene is in me, but it drifts. Sometimes it has taken the form of substance abuse. But other times it manifests behaviorally, in rule-breaking impulses that I seem to have sublimated away from explicit crime in favor of, for instance, small acts of resisting authority and institutions.

Still other times, my addiction manifests in the variety of ways I am a consumer, and that's another part to the story I'd like to give voice to. Today in America I'd say that there are whole armies of addicts out there in various states of recovery (or not) walking around trying to figure out what the hell happened and who the hell we are. In other words, to differing degrees, maybe all of us are losing control of our desires and behaviors a little at a time. We've become the things we buy. The gap between the outcasted, traditional back-alley junkie or weave-walking alcoholic and the rest of society is closing rapidly. The reason I think this conflation is important is that maybe it's time we recognize that our impulse to thrust the addict out and away from us as deviants or criminals and punishing their behavior is, you know, brutal and stupid. Maybe recovering addicts have something of use to share with a culture of people increasingly unaware that they are living for their own endless high.

I read a lot of articles and books on the topic of addiction, but not all of them stick. The ones that do tend to give it to me straight, no chaser in narrative form, in a story I can relate to because it includes me. In his article "Society of Addiction: Capitalism, Dopamine and the Consumer Junkie," Nicholas

Powers asks a good question: "If it's true that billions of people around the world are being addicted to our evolutionary Achilles' heel of salt, sugar, fat and status, then it's time to ask the question. Are we capitalism junkies?" He zeroes in on our BULK addictions to sugar, fat, fast food, to texting, to our beloved iPhones, our need to ever upgrade, our frenzied feeding on Facebook, Google, and Twitter. And what he locates in us is need. Big need. Like insatiable need, inextricably linked to very real ideas about dopamine, the same neurotransmitter involved in traditional drug addiction, usually associated with social outcasts like junkies, the poor, or people who break the law.

That need Powers so eloquently identifies corresponds directly to the stories we are telling ourselves these days about our own identities—that we will never be enough, have enough, to be worth something. That we've in fact lost self-worth to the glitz and sheen inherent in consumerism, as so aptly illustrated by the artist Barbara Kruger:

Summarizing from an earlier article written by Terrence Robinson and Kent Berridge, "Addiction," Powers goes on to say:

> There are two systems in the brain, one that involves dopamine based on wanting and the other based on liking, the opioid system, which gives us pleasure. The former says, "Go!" The latter says, "Stop and enjoy." But with social media, we now live in a culture where the "Go!" light is always green. In seconds we can text, Facebook, Google or call and get rewarded, which incites us to seek again, which rewards us again, causing us to seek again and be trapped in a dopamine loop.

The answer to his question "Are we capitalism junkies?" is yes.

So much yes.

And that means that the gap between our traditional notion of a junkie and the average gainfully employed and upwardly mobile individual is radically closing. Two words for you: pain meds.

So what do recovering addict misfits have to share with their new brothers and sisters?

For one thing, stop trying to jettison us away from you. We are you.

When I was so exhausted from the first two years of motherhood, the frantic breast-pumping in my office between teaching classes, the endless sleep deprivation that made me unable to drive in a straight line, the physically impossible multitasking of grading essays, cooking dinners, cleaning dishes, washing clothes, having sex, AND taking showers and dressing myself with my clothes on right-side out every day, so exhausted that

I sat in my car before my night classes drinking those terrible midget bottles of wine that you can buy in a four-pack at Safeway, I was you.

When my daughter died the day she was born and I ate an entire bottle of sleeping pills, I was you.

Even when I was passing as a college student sort of going to class but not much and partying like other college students and having three times the sex as other college students and numbing my body with heroin and alcohol because the rage and pain I was carrying around from father invasion home as a warzone was simply not the story anyone wanted to hear, I was you.

When I flunked out and didn't know where to put my anger and confusion except into having sex with increasingly dangerous people who showed me the door to needle-life, I was you.

Sitting in a jail cell for a DUI after nearly killing someone, I was you.

Living underneath an overpass with the ghost people you like to pretend you can't see, doing whatever I had to do just to keep breathing, I was you.

I'm the part of you that you don't want to admit is there. That's something I have to live with the rest of my life—the knowledge that I am capable of terrible things, even if I am also capable of good things. Tell me: Am I so very different from you? Admitting we are a part of each other interrupts the motion of trying to make me into something else, something darker than you or dirtier than you or weaker than you or less intelligent than you. And yet the people I have met who have fallen are not darker, or dirtier, or more weak, or less intelligent than any of us. They are us. Our paths make a helix.

What else can those of us in various states of recovery share with the rest of culture?

Misfits are remarkably good at reinventing a self when things don't go as planned, since we've had to do it so many times. Misfits can see beauty in weird, difficult, or hard things, and now more than ever we need to expand what we mean by "beauty" since we've incarcerated so many young women within its narrowest lines. Misfits can learn and show others how to see mistakes as portals; when you walk into jail you understand exactly what a closed door means. But when you walk out, my god. When you walk out? The whole world.

Misfits are pretty good at identifying when to leave a bad relationship—we see the warning signs very early. We know what's at stake. And misfits, well, I'd have to take a poll on this to be sure, but I suspect we know a great deal about the difference between usefulness to others and happiness that serves only the self.

My mother was an alcoholic and a suicide case. It's in me. But so is the drive to live, to find forms of expression that might help all of us see how much we are pieces of one another.

•   •   •

My friend Zach Ellis and I had a seemingly innocent lunch with each other about three years ago. We dined at a bistro about a block away from Powell's Books, where Zach worked at the time. I don't know where it came from, but while we were sitting there, I said, "In three years your life is going to look completely different." We were both a little miserable at the time, partly based on the ways in which our work lives were killing us, and partly on the way our past choices were haunting us. We were also both a little on the edge of choices that would change our lives. I didn't know it at the time, but that sentence was for me, too. All we had to do was finish standing up inside the stories we'd been writing about ourselves, which by the way, we both did.

I think of misfits as people who don't fit where others do. I think of misfits as people who got dealt an entirely different set of cards from everyone else and our job is to find the beauty in that deck. I finally don't want to fit in. I'm a misfit by circumstance, but have evolved into a misfit of choice.

I'm a misfit by circumstance and survival. I try to go from point A to point Z, but I usually end up taking a detour through points BFXNYT. It makes sense in my head, but not many other people's heads. Sometimes my world feels like an IKEA instruction book with no illustrations, from fifty years ago, and I'm the only one who never learned how to read Swedish. I compensate and try to find my way the best I can and hope no one notices. I know my thinking is very different. I have had to figure things out in my head that I know isn't the way "normal" people figure things out. I think I'm still that little kid who had no way to navigate shit and came up with the best possible solutions based on a very limited skill set.

How it felt to be that little kid was always anxious. My earliest memory of my mom was her throwing a big ceramic plate over my head when she was drunk. My father wasn't really around because he was always away writing for National Geographic. *My mother's priority has always been herself. She's the first to proudly admit she never wanted kids. When she got sober, her life was AA meetings anytime and anywhere, followed by her job, followed by parenting. My sister and I were dragged along to these meetings, which were always in a church basement, and told to shut up while the meeting was going on. If we talked or she felt like we would disturb the meeting, she would find a room in the church for us to play in. By ourselves. Do you have any idea how fucking creepy churches are at night? I would always play by myself because my sister was doing her best to take care of her own self. We were six and seven. I made up stories and had a whole host of invisible friends. I didn't know I was supposed to brush my teeth every day. I didn't know I was supposed to use soap when I took a bath. She would come home from AA meetings at 10 PM and wake us up to go to Baskin-Robbins for ice cream sundaes. She said life was all about being spontaneous. I didn't know vegetables were important and that sugar wasn't a food group. I had my first rotten tooth pulled before I was nine. I didn't know that wasn't normal. I could never relax because I never knew what was coming next. Things could change at any moment and it was better to be prepared than not. I was lonely because I was afraid to make friends. I peed in my pants until seventh grade because I was afraid to ask for something as simple as permission to use the bathroom. I was called Smellis Ellis by the kids in school and called "weirdo" a lot. I stopped relying on people and started relying on myself. I tried killing myself for the first time when I was ten, by trying to OD on my mother's Antabuse. I knew I wasn't doing things right, but no one ever told me how to do things differently. It was all about shaming me.*

I feel like a misfit in the way I see the world. The way I have to navigate through it. My story has a lot of survival. I was raised by people who had no business being parents. I wasn't taught basic skills, so had no idea I wasn't doing it "right" until I was around a lot of people who were doing it right, who pointed out just how wrong I was.

I identify as a man, a writer, and a dad. I feel like my life experiences have given me so many labels, but I'm so bored with having to pull them all out. There's a difference to me between being ashamed of labels and using them. I could say that I'm transgender, a recovering alcoholic, a former lesbian, a divorcee, an Arab American, and a not-able-bodied-although-it-looks-that-way man. I'm not ashamed of any of those things. They are all a part of me, but what's the point of pulling them out each time I meet someone or talk about myself? To make everyone feel better? Those things are all a part of who I am, but they don't go away if I just tell you I'm a man, a writer, and a dad. They come out in my writing, in my voice, in my life.

I've been in customer service all my work life. Right now, I'm a concierge at a hospital. I help people who are sick and lost. That's my paid job. I'm a writer, too. When I'm at the hospital, I get to use the best parts of myself. I don't know about other misfits, but because I haven't fit in in so many parts of life, I feel a real connection with people who are struggling. My heart opens. When you can really embrace all the parts of you that won't win you any awards— the ugly parts, the parts of you that make others cringe, the parts of you that you were always told are worthless—I believe you can see other people as human and have compassion. As a writer, I have found solace in expressing the ways I've survived and the ways I don't fit in. I started writing just for me, because I needed a way to express pain I had been carrying with me for a long time. The more I wrote, the more people would talk with me and tell me they related to what I was writing about. I love the feeling of knowing I'm not alone in the ways I feel different.

I parent two eight-year-old girls. I wouldn't describe either girl as a misfit, but I wouldn't count it out either. One is introverted, but not shy. The other is an extrovert. Both girls are awkward in the world. One is physical and forgets that not everyone is. The other is happy to spend hours reading and coming up with stories. One wants to be a feline biologist when she grows up, the other wants to be a social worker like her mom. I decided the best way I can parent these kids is to let them be interested in whatever they're interested in, and listen. Mostly listen when they are awkward, when they talk about things I don't understand. When they speak with passion about something I might not agree with. Listen as they try to navigate their own way in the world.

I look at the hundreds of mistakes I've made in my life as information. I mean, I look at it that way now. Most of the time I've just described myself as a fuckup because of how I've navigated through life.

Joining the navy twenty days after high school graduation because I was told I wouldn't do well in college (by my father), and pretty much drinking my way through four years of service. (Sub-mistake A: during my duty assignment in Iceland, when offered a chance to fly to Paris for a week on a $20 flight I decided I'd rather stay in my barracks and drink instead. Sub-mistake B:

having unprotected sex with whatever man didn't call me ugly. Sub-mistake C: getting pregnant and having to figure out what to do by myself. Sub-mistake D: developing an ulcer by the time I was twenty-one from alcohol abuse.)

When I started thinking of these mistakes as just information and part of my life story, I suddenly saw that I'd experienced a lot that not many other people had and the ones that could relate to me were the people I wanted to be around. When I stopped trying to be whatever I thought normal was, I started finding that the people I let into my life were pretty misfitty too. My partner and I connected by sharing about how much we felt as if we didn't fit in. I think that's one of the reasons we both feel so much love for each other. Because she's my home and I'm hers. We can be a safe place for each other. We don't always have to explain why we act or feel the way we do. I think that's what love is.

7 The Misfit's Journey, or, Why the Hero's Journey Bites

There's a story in most cultures that is meant to depict the drama of human experience. The hero's journey is an archetypal story pattern, common in ancient myths as well as modern-day adventures. The concept of the hero's journey was best described by mythologist Joseph Campbell in his book *The Hero with a Thousand Faces* and later adapted by Christopher Vogler in his book *The Writer's Journey*.

Here is a hilarious diagram of the hero's journey (I'll tell you why it's hilarious in a moment).

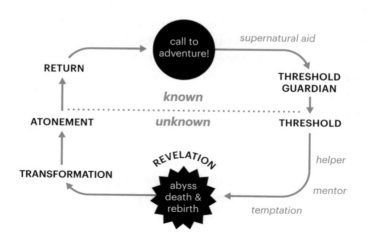

Forgive my cynicism, but what I love the most about this particular diagram and why it is hilarious to me is the exclamation point used at the end of "Call to Adventure!" As well as the weird little spiked outline surrounding "Abyss, Death, and Rebirth" ... like *Youch! Look out!* I can't help it. Put simply, the diagram cracks me up.

And yet, like me, if you look at the diagram long enough, you'll realize pretty quickly that this narrative pattern fits nearly every dramatic film, play, television series, novel, and even biblical or other sacred text you've ever seen, read, or heard in your life. In America in particular our mainstream and best-selling or blockbuster narratives fit this archetypal pattern fairly regularly. Harry Potter. Luke Skywalker. Jesus.

Before I go on, let me say that I have nothing but respect and reverence for the archetype and everyone everywhere who gave their life to the study of it and its manifestations—in history, philosophy, religion, art, archaeology, anthropology, etc.

My problem isn't with the hero's journey. My problem is with how we have commodified and consumed it in contemporary culture. My problem is how much the product of the original archetype has supersaturated our lived experiences. A person can witness the representations and productions of their culture and long for their own lives to be more like them. A person can even start living as if they can achieve the story version so that they don't have to live with the real-life version. But here's the thing: we fail. Worse, nonheroes and nonheroic behavior can get coded as "weak" or wrong, feminine or ugly, or failure, even though the notion of a "hero" in the first place is a construct.

Pure construct. When did we forget that we are not the stories we tell ourselves? How do we live our lives authentically when the stories have supersaturated and overtaken our selves?

Even though it's a terrific archetype and story line, some bodies don't fit the hero's journey. Women's lives, bodies, and experiences don't fit the archetypal hero's journey. Neither do the bodies, lives, and experiences of people of color. Neither Native Americans nor African Americans can track their mythos through this journey, for instance, since they were treated as the raw material through which the hero passed in order to forge a new world. Nor do the lives, bodies, and experiences of poor people, recovering (or not) addicts, people who struggle with mental health issues, prisoners, war veterans, or refugees. When you can be attacked and raped because you deigned to walk outside your door for a run; when you can be shot for reaching to retrieve your book in your own car or your own home or your license from your wallet or reaching for a pack of Skittles; when your sanity or economic status is viewed through the lens of mental instability whether you are mentally unstable or not, your body will not jam comfortably into the hero's journey. You are, more than anything, coded as a nonhero. Outside the hero's journey. Worse, you can be coded a villain. A witch. Evil.

While you can find some "revised" versions of the archetypal hero's journey in feminist and multicultural theory, as well as in art and literature, I'm more nettled by the idea that the archetype—as well as all the mainstream or blockbuster representations that have followed it and become our go-to for escape, entertainment, or catharsis—legitimizes some bodies and stories over others.

What I'm saying is, there's a myth to following your dreams that we've inherited, knowingly or not. It's called the hero's journey. But there's also a myth slightly to the side or under-neath those success stories. It's the misfit's myth. It goes like this: Even at the moment of your failure, you are beautiful. You may not know this yet, but you have the ability to endlessly make yourself up from your own ruins. That's your beauty.

In the plot of the hero's journey, there seems to be a kind of magical forward momentum implied. If misfits could just push through the stages in order! Whereas in the misfit's myth, the stages are all mixed up, on top of each other, with false doors and creepy basements and Escheresque stairwells. (I'd draw you a diagram but I don't want to frighten anyone.) And you can find versions of it everywhere, too. For example, at the base of the Statue of Liberty:

"The New Colossus"

Not like the brazen giant of Greek fame,
With conquering limbs astride from land to land;
Here at our sea-washed, sunset gates shall stand
A mighty woman with a torch, whose flame
Is the imprisoned lightning, and her name
Mother of Exiles. From her beacon-hand
Glows world-wide welcome; her mild eyes command
The air-bridged harbor that twin cities frame.

> "Keep, ancient lands, your storied pomp!" cries she
> With silent lips. "Give me your tired, your poor,
> Your huddled masses yearning to breathe free,
> The wretched refuse of your teeming shore.
> Send these, the homeless, tempest-tossed to me,
> I lift my lamp beside the golden door!"

While many of us recognize those last few lines, I don't know how many American people can name the author of this poem. Her name was Emma Lazarus, and she wrote the poem for a fund-raiser auction to raise money for the pedestal on which Lady Liberty sits.

Read that poem again.

It's actually a quite clear critique of the tradition of the male hero's journey, with his "conquering limbs astride from land to land," and in its place, at the bottom of things, sits a different story, one in which Liberty turns into a welcoming mother, a symbol of hope to the outcasts and downtrodden of the world. You can keep your storied pomp. She wants the outcasts, the downtrodden, the immigrants, and I would argue, us misfits.

In fact, if you look hard enough, you can find alternatives to the hero's journey all over the world. However, for a variety of reasons, the hero's journey has risen as a primary monomyth over other kinds of journey stories.

Before I get accused of taking anyone's hero away from them, let me be clear. Heroes are great. I sit and eat popcorn right next to all the other moviegoers and cheer when the hero overcomes difficulties and enemies. But even if I can be entertained by their stories, I just don't identify with them. Here's another secret: a lot of us are also secretly empathizing with the so-called villain. I've been arrested. I've gone to jail and rehab. I'm no hero. But every fall I've taken has shown me how to be a better person. Profoundly.

My life is filled with flaws and mistakes. Some of the obstacles I have encountered were of my own making; some came from the outside and were out of my control, such as my father's abuse. I haven't particularly risen above anything, but I am still standing. I hope I've learned from my mistakes but I also know I will make them again. I suspect I am not alone in this.

Since I was born into an abusive household, I started out in hell, like so many other people on the planet. I had to find and invent escape hatches just to keep from killing myself. That doesn't really fit the trajectory of the hero's journey. I numbed myself in waves with drugs, or sex, or self-destructive behaviors just to ease the pain of failing at ordinary social paths: college, marriage, motherhood, employment. Flunked out, twice divorced, dead child, fired twice. I can admire the hero's journey, but it has never taken shape in my life. For this reason, all the stories I tell have a weird shape to them. And yet, might those new shapes speak to someone besides just me? Might someone else's weird-story shapes make my life a little easier to bear? Where are the stories that might welcome us home in our imperfection?

•   •   •

The first time I met my friend Melanie Alldritt, she showed up in a class she was not signed up for and asked if she could stay.

I mean she infiltrated. I instantly liked her, in part because the very first creative writing class I entered was also an act of infiltration. In my early twenties after I'd flunked out of college in Texas, I moved to Boston, where my sister was attending Brandeis University. I took a shitty job at a clothing store in Harvard Square. And during my lunch hour I snuck into creative writing classes at Harvard. It took them several weeks to identify me as an interloper. But those weeks were glorious. So when Melanie showed up in my fiction writing class, I said what I always say. Stay.

Melanie's story is the kind that gives me an alternative kind of hopefulness. A hope forged not from looking up or transcending difficulty or being saved, but rather from her own agency and imagination barreling through reality, refusing to surrender. You might say she has used her body as a battering ram against the walls her culture built around her. And yet from the wreckage of her life mistakes she still builds a story. I identify with that idea. Stories can be any shape in the world. Misfit stories take all kinds of forms. This is Melanie's story about herself:

Having some quirks or odd habits does not make you a misfit. A person can insist on wearing socks with pom-poms and platform boots every day of their life and still move through it in the way that is socially acceptable and expected without much issue. A misfit is a person who, either through who they are or what they've experienced, can't make it through the smooth way. They fuck up or have to find a weird way that makes sense to nobody else but them. Maybe it looks crazy from the outside. Or maybe their frustrations look like failures to other people. Something in them won't allow the smooth, easy way. But even misfits need some fucking community. The person who wears socks with pom-poms on them every day and I aren't going to understand each other, but I understand a person who can't look someone in the eye because they are terrified. I also understand how that fear creates a string that every decision and experience in a life is woven around. That is the community I both want and need. Misfits don't judge one another. Ever.

As a kid I was a hella poor brown girl who was intelligent, competitive, and antagonistic. Because of the intelligent part I took honors classes. Unfortunately, as a kid and teen who was doing a lot of drugs, had poor attendance, and had a life that was a series of explosive things and explosive people, I did not fit well into that community. The last day I showed up to Latin American History my teacher yelled at me for forty minutes about my inconsistencies and failures. He went on to win important awards, met the president, and is a prestigious dude. My senior year I got kicked out of half my classes because of the drugs and the attendance and the not-being-a-typical-honor-student thing. My work was impeccable but inconsistent. I heard a lot about my potential and how I was not living up to it. I still hear that. I fucking hate that sentence and the word potential.

As an adult I am not entirely sure what is going on half the time, to be honest, but I can detect some patterns. I know that when shitty things happen I have no feelings for a little bit and then I go make a mess. I know that when love is on the line I'll go pretty damn far. I know that my scale of "don't do that because it's of course wrong" is not the same as most people's. I think the life I was born into, if I had gone along with what is expected of poor brown women, would have killed me. If I look at myself I can see that I am largely a product of trauma and surviving it. Traumatic experience reverberates. I am either intensely passionate or indifferent. I am not good at doing things I don't care about. But I care about people; I care even more about people who are trying really hard to make it through life, and I am good at meeting them where they're at. Even if that place is on the streets or in a drug house or on the edge of their life. I'm okay with going to these places because I know I am equipped to survive in ways most people are not. I often find the edges of things unconsciously and don't pick up on it until the edges are cutting my feet. But I've got a lot of thick scars so I try to have some faith. I'm guessing my faith doesn't look like other people's faith.

In my childhood, emotions were a liability. My mother has some mental health issues and trying to be there as a four- or five-year-old broke me. Dealing with the feelings involved in trying, small-child-style, to take care of her made me want to die. And then so many other shitty things happened in quick succession and my life kept changing and something below cognition in my brain figured out that the way to keep moving through it all was to not have feelings. I know completely that the ability to turn off my emotions and physiological responses and, to some extent, memory is how I've made it here.

I also know that this mentality, "dissociation" as shrinks like to call it, is completely born of trauma for me. I just stay unfeeling and without memory until difficulty passes, but what transpires in that period of not feeling can be catastrophic.

I can put my body in the face of great risk of physical harm and not blink an eye or have any fear. I can put myself in front of violent things and people and not have any feelings about it. I look back on some places I've put myself and don't have feelings about them still. But people, the people I love, children, people I know and feel to be fundamentally good, scare the living shit out of me. People who say good things to me scare the living shit out of me. They also piss me off. You can tell me I'm poison and should go kill myself and I won't care, but say you love me and think I'm talented and I will want to punch you in the face and run away. Also I won't actually hear a damn word of the good. I think people would say that's a flaw, a problem I have. And yeah, it is, and I promise I'm working on it with my shrink, but it's also a strength. You need people like me in dangerous situations. But when the danger passes, you find fault with people like me.

Look, if you are like me, I'm not going to tell you that one day you'll be happy or be able to look yourself in the mirror and see your worth or that you won't want to die. I don't know if any of those things are true. But you're here, and you are going to continue to be here, and a way to make being alive and in the world easier is to find a thing you need to do. Something you need to do badly enough that doing it makes you so present that nothing else matters for a little while. It can be anything you invent. Hopefully not something that will land you a prison sentence or harm another being. For me those things are helping people, climbing things, and making art. Even when I don't want to be alive, which is honestly most of the time, or when I look in the mirror and see a worthless fuckup, which is also most of the time, while I do these things not a single thought between my ears matters. Because other people matter, and I get to help them. Because art matters, and I get to create it. And climbing things shrinks the scope of my brain to only what is in front of me. And even if it doesn't last long after, these things make me happy. Especially the helping people one. ANYONE can do this. You get back so much of what you give. You can believe yourself to be a worthless piece of crap that doesn't deserve to be alive and still you can help people. For me, for a long time, helping people has been how I earn my seat at the table of life. Helping people worked then and it still does now no matter what.

Also if you hang out long enough, if you only do the bare minimum to keep alive, something will happen that is important: your life will be your own. It may change everything or nothing, it will be fantastic or terrible or ugly, it will or will not make you happy, but that is something worth sticking around for. It's a transition and feeling I can't describe but I can say that if it hadn't happened to me I wouldn't be able to feel a single good thing that has happened to me in my adult life. While I'm not always happy to be alive, I am grateful that I stuck around long enough for my life to become mine. I didn't actually know that was a "thing" until now.

In 2014 I jumped off a cliff. There are many ways to look at that sentence. I'm fairly experienced as a rock climber, so one way to look at it is that I fell. Another way would be to say that I jumped. All I can say for sure is that it seemed like what I should do at the time.

If I were a television character I'd definitely be Jessica Jones. Only brown.

When I was falling, the only thought I had was "this is the end of my life" and that gave me a lot of peace. Except for the fact that

I didn't actually die. Years before that I had eaten a bottle of pills, there were a couple of overdoses, and a time that I nicked an artery and had to go to the hospital for stitches and an awkward conversation with an awkward resident psychiatrist. The cliff incident was different in that I actually started to think about why I kept making those kinds of choices.

As an adolescent I had this idea that I was not good enough. It's what poor brown girls are told, girls who go through trauma, girls who are the targets of rage, girls who want to die. I still often think I am not enough. Or too much. As an adolescent my way of making myself the right size was to lie. A lot. So much that I now have a tattoo on my left forearm as a reminder because I was on drugs and dishonest and let a person down. I think of that relationship often. I look at that tattoo often. Their favorite flower.

One night in my midtwenties I did acid, ate shrooms, drank, smoked weed, and then tried to drive myself and one of my best friends across three cities to her home in the middle of the night. It's blatantly obvious that this was an incredibly stupid choice, but I was pissed and loaded and it made sense at the time. The fact that she loved me the next morning taught me the power of love, the value of love, and also not to fuck with it. It taught me that I had grown enough and that maybe I was brave and vulnerable enough to let a fellow misfit in so far that she has become necessary to me. People are necessary and so is love. I never thought I'd see the day. It's not the definition of love I learned from my culture or school, that's for sure.

I learn things without knowing them and then make a big fat blunder and realize "OH SHIT, I'm different." *I learn change*

*through blunders. I wish I didn't, but right now that is where I
am. Maybe blunders are knowledge. Maybe that's something I
have to give.*

A beautiful girl survived the hell of her own life by running
toward self-destruction. She was on drugs and she was dishonest and let down someone she loved. But she also learned how
to make stories, and art, how to change self-destruction into
expression. She doesn't get it right all the time. None of us do.
But her story makes me feel like trying again.

Oh how I wish our lives were just like a movie that followed
the script of the hero's journey. But I've been waiting for over
half a century for the "transcend" part . . . it never comes. Turns
out, more difficulty just circles back around, usually something
I'm familiar with only in a different form. I remember when I
was in the pit of despair after my second divorce—and when I
say "pit of despair" I mean not bathing for weeks, not changing
clothes, my hair matting into a nest, half-eaten food all over
the house, lights off, TV perpetually on, bawling every exhale,
jumbo wine and vodka bottles strewn about—I wondered what
the hell was wrong with me that I couldn't transcend my pain
and emerge in some beautifully transformational moment—
with theme music and excellent lighting! What was wrong with
me that I couldn't transcend, but rather only learn maybe a
thimbleful more about how life is chaos at best, that our hearts
accumulate scar tissue if we choose to stay alive through a
series of literal and figurative deaths, and that while we love
to have beautiful forms and stories in our lives because they

make us feel better and less afraid, we're just temporary beings struggling to become as much as we can with the time we've got on the planet we're fast destroying. That some of us give up and die and that isn't any better or worse than those of us who keep going in all the different ways we choose to do so. That those who keep going might use faith, while the person right next to them might use drugs and alcohol, and the person next to that one might use the high or thrill of adrenaline, and the person next to that one might use sex or making art or a life-long military career or becoming a mother or healing the sick or chasing fame. And always the homeless person, who started out, of course, as us, is standing next to all of us. In short, there are a million different paths with a million different tributaries along the way culminating in a million different stories, half stories, fragmented stories, contradictory stories, anything but a monostory. No one's life perfectly "fits" the monostory just because it exists and recurs in our culture or our history. Not the hero's journey or the happily-ever-after story of marriage or the skyward story of faith or the socially sanctioned stories of death or love, love worst of all, because for all of us, when it comes to love, there is nothing but misfitting.

And the beauty of that.

The wonder.

8 Bodies that Don't Fit

If I track back through my own jagged life stories looking for my misfit origins, I think for me at least part of the story might have been born with my mother's leg.

My mother was born with one leg six inches shorter than the other. Her limp was considerable. The scar running up her leg mesmerized me as a child, white-pearled and risen. She had to have her shoes specially made, so one shoe always had a strange and fascinating false heel to it. She wore very stylish shoes. She was a successful real estate agent. Not something you'd expect from someone with a severe limp and lifelong pain in her hip. All that walking from empty home to empty home, all that standing around at open houses.

No one in my household ever used the word *disabled* or *disability*. I didn't even learn that word until I was in high school, or maybe I just didn't pay attention to it until then. My mother refused to get a disability-parking placard. She refused to use a cane for as long as possible. She'd just wince with every step, until that wince became part of her smile and Southern drawl.

My paternal grandmother once called her a "cripple," and that word hung like blasphemy in the shadows of our house. When she recalled that moment her small blue eyes would widen and gleam—ready to shoot out like a Texas bullet, if necessary.

She was born in Port Arthur, Texas, raised on secrets and lies and oil rigs and dirt and heat and anything anything anything to get out.

Anything turned out to be my Yankee father from Ohio.

I've thought a lot about what it meant to me. Her leg I mean. Her extreme physical difficulty. I've thought about how she couldn't ride a bike or run or ride a horse. When I learned to drive a stick shift I thought about how she couldn't, since her hip and right leg were too stiff to accomplish the moves. I've thought about how many times my father took us hiking and camping, and what that must have felt like to her, and how I never once heard her complain or reveal what must have been excruciating pain. I've wondered what the look on her face was when a doctor told her not to risk having children.

Mostly I've thought about how she begged me to come live with her after I was an adult, when she wanted to have her hip replaced and reconstructive surgery on her leg. I've swum the deep waters of how I said no. I've thought about the kind of ferocity it took to live her life. To bear two children when doctors told her we'd be crushed by the crooked canal formed by her hips. To win award after award for selling houses as a successful real estate agent. All that walking and standing. To feign fashion and beauty with a limp like that. To endure her husband, my father, our abuser. To watch her daughters leave the house. Forever.

You'll think it's weird how much I loved her leg. As a child I mean. I think I may have fetishized it. I dreamed about it, I thought about it at school during the day, I replayed how I would sit in the bathroom every morning and achingly watch her put makeup on, half-dressed in her bra and panties, her skin still flushed and glistening from the shower. I have very specific knowledge of this strange sacred space we shared. She wore, for example, a 38C bra. Her underwear was always nylon and covered her belly, which she was self-conscious of due to two cesarean scars railroading across her abdomen. And yet not so self-conscious that she'd keep her daughter out of the bathroom while she got ready for work.

Her leg though, that was the thing of beauty. I guess because I was a kid, and thus short, it was ever eye level, and the vertical line crosshatched with horizontal lines long as my thumb? Well, the lines on her leg did me in.

To this day I think odd or wrong or dead things are more beautiful than the beauty everyone else seems to marvel at.

When I say I dreamed about it, I mean it came to life differently.

In my dreams, her leg had special powers. It was magical. You know, the way kids believe in things like that. With all of their heart and maybe their whole body.

Up until I read a short story by Flannery O'Connor in college.

"Good Country People" is a short story about a woman named Joy Hopewell, whose PhD in philosophy leads her to a complete denial of her Christian faith. Due to a hunting accident in her childhood, Joy loses her leg and is forced to use an artificial one. What is more, she has poor eyesight and suffers from some kind of heart condition that puts her life at risk and prevents her from realizing an academic career. She has to live in her childhood house with her mother and their meddlesome tenant, growing more sullen and harsh every day. She even changes her positive-sounding name to a really horrible one—Hulga. One day, a Bible salesman named Manley Pointer appears and manages to win Hulga's trust; however, he soon proves to be an even greater cynic than Hulga, and an utterly cruel creature that does not hesitate to steal the disabled woman's artificial limb.

To me, the leg was an allegorical representation of O'Connor's own illness, lupus, which forced her to live in her mother's care as an adult on the family farm and kept her from participation in the intellectual life found in big cities. The wooden leg stands as a perfect symbol of limitation and restriction, and ultimately O'Connor's incapacitation by lupus.

I'm not saying I'm proud of this, but Joy Hopewell is the reason I said no when my mother asked me to come home to live with her while she convalesced. She wanted surgery. She'd raised her children, one with a PhD, my older sister, one on her way to her own PhD, me, both out in the world safely away from our father's abuse. Now she wanted her life back. She wanted out. I wanted a life of the mind, away from what had been done to my body, by any means necessary. I wanted to be a writer. It took everything I had to get out.

And there was no way I was going to die in that Oedipal house of my father, leg or no leg.

It's almost like I stole her leg.

When I look back now, I see the shades of my cruelty. I do.

Maybe if I'd been raised in the South, I would have gone back to help her. Maybe immediately and without question. The South has a way of breeding ritual and rules into a woman in a way that nowhere else does. But I was born in San Francisco, because my mother left her family to follow my father. She was the only one to do so. When her mother told her to come back home, she said no. Over and over again, she ran. In an unsyncopated lope. So maybe I'm my mother's daughter after all.

I did not come home when she asked me to nor anytime thereafter, except when she had stage-four cancer and I had a newborn son. I did not take care of her then, either, though I thought about it very hard, and decided I could not trade his life for hers.

You may think I sound cold. Maybe I am cold. And yet there is more inside the story.

When I was sixteen, I came home from high school in Florida where we lived at the time and flopped down on our living room couch. My mother was not selling real estate at that point. She was barely getting dressed each day. She was mind-numbingly depressed; she'd survived a serious suicide attempt the previous year, and she drank every afternoon and night. Either rum or vodka mixed drinks. She sat on the couch watching soap operas every day in place of living a life.

I didn't want to talk about this, which is why I blew past it in the previous paragraph—did you see it? her suicide attempt— so I'll go back to where I don't want to go so that you can see something about people like me. I'm the person who was with my mother the previous summer in Florida, when I was fifteen, when she ate an entire bottle of sleeping pills with a vodka chaser. We were alone in the house together. At the time, I freaked out, called my sister in Massachusetts, then called an ambulance, and lastly, my father at work.

When I look back at that piece of the story now, I'm not freaked out. I'm the age now that she was then. I've faced the cusp of giving up and giving in, more than once. I've faced the "enough" edge. I've been in the bad marriage, not once, but twice. I've submerged myself in a sea of vodka. I've made enough bad choices to fill a pool. So now when I look back I think maybe she trusted me enough to understand that she truly wanted to die, and to not let her die, but to just see that place—between living and dying—and to see that it is real—even though yes, that is an unfair thing to do to a fifteen-year-old girl. And yet, compared to what I had already endured from my father, it was not something I couldn't face. In fact, I would face several more life-death moments in my life to come. Life and death are never at two ends of a magical rope. They make an endless palimpsest.

I know. It sounds like I'm saying that my mother's suicide attempt was something important she gave to me.

I wonder what it would be like to let that be true.

Later in life, the year after her suicide attempt, what she did that day when I was sixteen, in the living room, from her submerged state, was hand me a newspaper clipping. "I think you should do this," she said.

The newspaper clipping described a local writing contest.

After school every day for a month, instead of watching soap operas and slugging vodka, she sat with me on the couch and talked with me until a story came out of me. Though I can see now that part of the story was her.

I won.

The local writing contest. Though I would not understand that there was a writer in me for many, many more years.

For a very long time I've held my mother responsible for not saving us from my abusive father. Not getting us out of there. Now that I'm on this side of saving myself and living a different family story, I can see that she also gave her two daughters an ungodly and beautiful gift: knowing that we could walk into the world alone, as women, and re-story ourselves. In the face of anything.

My mother was a misfit. Flannery O'Connor was a misfit. I'm a misfit. I think about her now and how she is in every word I will ever write, though she died before she reached seventy. My mother gave writing to me like a secret I held in my body for a decade. For better or worse, I took it and ran.

Not for nothing am I talking about the body. For some misfits, our bodies carry the evidence of what went wrong in our lives. Our pasts show up on our skin or in our guts, in my crooked-as-a-question-mark scoliosis spine or in chronic pain that never leaves. In the way we understand our own edges, physically, emotionally, psychologically, and just how far we'll go to protect those edges.

For misfits, our bodies are sites of resistance.

•   •   •

My friend and creative colleague Domi Shoemaker helps me re-member every day how to respect the ways in which our actual bodies carry profound life stories. The first time I met Domi we arranged for an illicit drive-by book signing. That is, Domi attended one of my readings, and then arranged for us to meet so that I could sign some books they wanted to give to a friend. Due to my crazy work schedule, we agreed that Domi would drive by someplace I was at and I'd jump in their car, sign the books, exit, and they'd speed away. It was a hilarious encounter. It was also a life-changing one, since a year later we'd be co-facilitating my nonacademic workshop series that we called Corporeal Writing. Domi helped me realize my dream to bring writing and artistic practice out of academia and into the world for every mind and every body. This is their story:

I definitely identify with the word misfit. *I grew up poor in a small middle-class town in a very large body with secondhand clothes.*

Plastic bread bags and basement house. My style and gender representation fluctuated and was generally inconsistent with the gender norms of my time and place. I'm making that sound like no big deal. It was a BIG DEAL. Ha. Literally. In my earlier years, I took that energy and fought back and became something of a bully before I realized in fourth grade that hurting other people didn't feel so hot.

I turned to humor and made myself somewhat of a clown, so if I was going to be noticed, it was going to be on my terms, and not a label someone else slapped on me.

I think everyone wants to be acknowledged as a misfit. They want to be recognized for their own unique brand of pain or suffering (or joy and enlightenment). But there is a real difference between being unique and being a misfit. Misfits don't really fit in anywhere. Or outwardly they may have developed a coping mechanism to seemingly fit in everywhere, but in a superficial way. As an extroverted misfit, I can work to seem like I fit in, because I talk and put on a show of sorts. It isn't false, but I am never really communicating from a real place. I am communicating from a place that makes me want to make YOU feel comfortable. I sort of erase myself.

I am definitely a misfit by both circumstance—andro/gender nonconforming, abuse-fighting survivor of all kinds of violence, sexual, physical, psychological—and choice. I say by choice because honestly? It would cost me too much emotionally to be like other people.

The story of me is one about a kid growing up in a place where conformity is rewarded. As much as I wanted to "fit in," it was my choice to say no in trying to conform, because it was too painful. So was it really a choice? Sometimes I think if I had tried harder to fit in, I might actually be dead.

I think this is a huge part of the conversation, because while it might be ME who makes the choice to alter my appearance, to say the things I want to say, to be me, it did not seem like I had a choice. To NOT do so made me susceptible to crippling depression and attempted suicide. I got into a lot of trouble early on with missing curfew, drinking, drugs, a ton of sex, etc. all in trying to figure out who I was.

When it came right down to it, I was a big queer kid in Idaho who was neither a girl nor a boy. Try fitting into THAT.

I wonder if it is the circumstance that makes it feel imperative?

Like the outward manifestation of my inner turmoil is pretty obvious in my hairstyle, piercings, etc. To be any other way is actually VERY uncomfortable. So maybe I accentuate my misfitting rather than hide it? Like punk rockers. An outward extreme expression of inward truths.

My mental health relies on my ability to express myself the way I need to. I have Dissociative Identity Disorder, and one way I have found to relieve anxiety is to change my appearance. I keep getting hung up on actual appearance, but it's not just that. It's the struggle to have my insides and outside match. I do think that people with mental health stuff experience unique kinds of misfit status and do experience things differently, depending on the type of mental illness and how much it impacts the ability to communicate ideas.

Some people pathologize and try to use diagnostic labels and snap people into categories, instead of seeing the possibilities. Any number of psychological conditions can be the basis of a creation, and can simultaneously create confusion and fear, both for the person and people around them. The general public seems terrified of mental health stuff, like they can be infected by it, like a contagion. They also don't know what to do and so mainly they are full of platitudes or are distant, which really doesn't help or makes things worse. Depends on the diagnosis and how much it impacts your life, your art, your ideas. On another side of a seven-sided dice, some people, like [Jean-Michel] Basquiat, are recognized for their artistic contributions but are elevated to a level that is not sustainable and actually causes more pain for the artist. Either way, the common denominator is there is certain erasure and dismissal of the person inside the artist.

About life paths, I say to youth that we all have inside us something that makes us excited or something that interests us, and I like to help look for and bring out that light. When I work with youth who are having a rough time, it is often because they haven't really found that thing that guides them and they already see their lives as a series of epic failures. I really want kids to know that whatever led them to where they are standing right now is a part of them and even if it was awful shit, it can be rich and essential information for them to build on. I don't say it in those words. The most important thing is to listen. Especially when talking to someone who is having a tough time of feeling like an outsider. Listen, share stories, share experiences, and create art. You know.

My multitude of life blunders—yeah. Some of the most difficult and fundamental transformation only comes by learning lessons from our mistakes, and if we aren't willing to risk everything (and embracing being a misfit is one way) and ask the deeper questions of ourselves in relation to the world and people around us, it's just jacking off into a jar.

I actually started smoking at age six or seven, weed at nine, alcohol at fourteen, then speed and coke and shrooms and acid. Pretty much everything but downers, and I never used a needle.

I fought a lot in grade school. Mostly boys. Protecting girls. All my fights were about protecting girls. Hmmm. Never thought of it like that. But yeah, I would have been called a juvenile delinquent, but I was also on the honor roll and class clown and played sports. I was the first girl allowed on the baseball team.

I didn't find my way out of all that until my late thirties. My self-destruction was actually part of my mind-set, like anybody who didn't do that stuff was a wuss, but at the same time I would idealize self-destruction. And that is the shame and guilt that poverty ground into me. I felt ashamed and guilty because I was poor. I acted out to seem tough. But self-destruction only looks cool on the outside.

One thing I know for sure is that I have ALWAYS been drawn to the humanity in people. I made friends with some of the supposedly meanest, baddest people, and it became almost a thing for me. Kinda shitty, maybe, because sometimes I would just do it to see if I could and turned that into a risky behavior. More than once I could have been killed. One of those people ended up on America's Most Wanted, then on another one of those shows when she ended up on a killing spree that ended in a murder-suicide.

At the same time I was flirting with danger I became a bouncer. Always trying to be the good guy of the bad guys. Always a conduit between conflicting cliques. Always used my sense of humor with the "good guys" (cops, teachers, detectives, and later FBI) and my muscle and anger with the "bad guys."

But those behaviors seem to me to be part of the process by which I transformed shame and guilt. That's my life's work now! To encourage other people to melt shame and fear and own it as part of what made them the beautiful misfit they are. We all are. Shame and fear are not the end of things. They are the beginning, if you let them become portals, which is why I like working with you, because you said that. The day you said that, my ears popped.

The bodies we inhabit are a bit like metaphors for all experience. Which bodies count in a culture; how and why? Which bodies are dismissed or maligned or incarcerated or harmed? Misfits have relationships to their own bodies in ways that map out some of the cultural fractures we come from. Big bodies or brown or black bodies, bodies beaten or belittled, bodies with differing abilities or bodies eating themselves alive . . . misfit bodies live at the edge of things.

Then again, the edges are where all new meanings are generated.

9 Mistakes as Portals

"What exactly is the matter with you?"

It's a question that still clatters around in my skull like dice in a cup sometimes. Why can't I go to social engagements without having a panic attack and hiding out in the laundry room of someone else's home, dryer wipes the most comforting smell on earth? Why can't I manage to follow basic social rules of behavior? Why do institutions piss me off so much? Why does male authority make me want to throw up or fight to the death? Why do I make a mess exactly when things are finally looking ordered?

A cop asked me that question the night he drove me from the scene of a car accident to jail. I was a college professor. I was no kid, I was approaching middle age. I had everything going for me. And yet I blew a number out of orbit on the Breathalyzer that night. It was a long ride. The look in his eyes in the rearview said, *Aren't you old enough to be someone's mother?* He could have been one of my grad students.

No one likes to self-narrate their biggest blunders in life; it's not a lot of fun to zoom in on the ways in which we blow up our own lives. On the other hand, misfits have a unique relationship to their own failures. If we are lucky, we come to understand them as portals. You heard me, portals. As in a doorway, gate, or other entrance, an opening.

One of my first major failures in life was flunking out of college. I was in Lubbock, Texas, on a swimming scholarship at Texas Tech University. Go Red Raiders. The first year I was in college I was so goddamn thrilled to be away from the horrors of home that I think I may have been in shock, in retrospect. I went to swim practice diligently, and for at least the first half of the year, I went to classes like a normal person. But something about my newfound freedom opened a crack inside me, like a fault line in the earth, only this fault line was my body. And from within that fissure came everything I'd been holding in for about eighteen years. In a way it felt like being released from prison, only I was free from family and father. In other words, to survive my own childhood I couldn't allow myself to feel the intensity of my emotions, because I thought I'd die from them. When the emotions came, later, when I was safe, I was flooded. Rage, fear, pain, confusion. What the hell was I supposed to do with those feelings? I had no idea. None whatsoever. No one or nothing in my life had coached me on how to cope with the monstrous feelings now coming out of me. The only coaching I'd had was the swim coach kind, and though that probably saved my life, it didn't do much to help my mental and emotional health. I felt like my hair was on fire and my skin was coming apart. So I just stopped going to classes regularly, and then I skipped practice sessions, and then I became something like an improvised explosive device.

I think as I look back on my young adult, entering college self, what I see quite obviously now is that I needed help. But I didn't know anything about needing help. All I knew about was achieving escape, and when I landed in freedom, I was lost. I'd simply used every ounce of energy I had to get out. In some ways I was like an eight-year-old set loose in the new world of sex, drugs, knowledge, and experience; since my development was likely arrested, but my body was blooming, I forged ahead the only way I knew how. A kind of human physics: my body and forward momentum. I threw myself into experiences without thought. My body was the only thing I had, and she was finally mine. I simply hadn't met my mind yet. I didn't even know she existed.

So yes, I plowed forward like a comet into sex and drugs, and one way to read that story is to say, well, that's a path so many young adults fall into, isn't it a shame, having had bad parenting or some kind of rebellious streak in them, or maybe they're just plain irresponsible, immature, a bad apple. They need to be taught a lesson. But I'm here to suggest that another way to read that story of a body is to see that I was desperately searching for a form of expression that might contain my rage, sadness, pain, and confusion. I was looking for someplace to put it, because though I didn't realize it yet, I was beginning to feel the effects of just how close you can come to dying from the inside out when you hold those things in. Maybe my entry into sex and drugs and skipping classes and breaking rules was not the story of another young adult screwup. Maybe I was looking for a language to channel a girl who lived inside me who was screaming her head off, raging her guts out.

In this liminal state of young womanhood, I made a second colossally bad choice. I got married. I hope that you can see the good-citizen script I was, in my own awkward and terrible way, still trying to follow. Women left home, went to college, got married, had children. Right? That's the story we're handed out in the world—every magazine, every television show, every movie, every woman who walked ahead of us. Even when an alternative image or person emerges that deviates from that plotline, we're often scared to follow it, because what if the world rejects us or treats us as unlikable because we chose something off script? That cultural message is alive and well today. I know because I teach college-aged women. In women's studies classes, film classes, writing classes, literature classes, whole oceans of women come in carrying that tired old script of how to be a woman, and that dangerous fear that you have no place in culture unless you do what you're told. I know because of how quickly women feel slighted on Facebook if they do not achieve enough "likes" or attention.

I was nineteen. I was not the kind of nineteen-year-old who was anywhere near capable of understanding what the responsibilities or conditions of being married meant. I'm now fifty-three and on my third marriage, and I'm just discovering what they mean. Shockingly, my marriage ended in divorce within three years. At the tail end of those three years, I got pregnant, and this sad little hope ignited in me that said, *Okay, you messed up the first part of the story, but you get a new chance to be a woman because you are going to have a baby.*

My beautiful little girl died the day she was born, as I've mentioned, and so, in a way, my story breached forever. The grief that came from that experience wrenched me out of the traditional womanhood plotline forever. The depression I entered was unholy.

And yet.

As I've narrated, from my daughter's death, eventually, I became a writer. It did not happen overnight. In fact, it took roughly ten years and another failed marriage, but when I look back, I can see that it was true. The first failed marriage, the first failed motherhood, they weren't *just* horrible failures. They were portals. Even if they felt like deadly crucibles at the time. But it would take me years to learn to see them that way.

Another of my more spectacular failures came in the shape of a DUI. This is an identifiable pattern of mine, if you track back through my past. I'm often at some kind of zenith of good when I do something that brings the whole shebang down. At the time, I was a visiting writer at San Diego State University, which given my past, was not nothing. I had divorced my second husband who, turns out, was a philandering schmoe, even though he was also dangerous and exciting for about eleven years. I had published two books of short stories. I'd gone back to school and emerged with a PhD, as unlikely as that sounds. I was teaching graduate students and undergraduate students. I lived a block from the ocean. It was almost as if my life was moving toward that foreign word, *successful*.

Yup, you guessed it. I made a new mess.

Now before you dismiss me as just another incapable person, someone to give up on because their mistakes are perpetual, hear me out. Though I'm the one who left the eleven-year marriage with my second, dangerous, exciting, alcoholic husband, I still had love in me. At that time in my life, I loved him more than I'd ever loved anyone or anything, and since I suspected that a person like me wouldn't ever deserve real love, the fact that I experienced it with my whole body and soul made leaving it tantamount to cutting off my own arms, gouging out my heart, leaving them in the dirt, and driving away in a shitty pickup with a busted taillight. Yeah. Armless. Heartless. Into the night. In other words, excruciating.

As a person who came from a childhood where "love" was a distorted fiction, and a young adult who tried to kill her own desire with sexuality, I'd finally risked loving someone or something and look where it got me.

So when my second husband called me in San Diego from Paris, the city where our love had taken hold and supernovaed, to tell me that he and his new girlfriend were having matching rings tattooed on their ring fingers, and he decided it was important to mention that she reminded him of me at twenty-three, well, all those clichés—a kick to the gut, a knife in the heart, a soul murder—all of them. I couldn't breathe that night when I hung up the phone. I walked into the bathroom. I looked in the mirror. I seriously considered cutting a line across my face and slitting my own throat. I entered that old familiar numbness of don't-know-who-I-am or how-to-be-in-the-world. So when I say I drank an entire bottle of vodka, got in my car, and drove as fast as I could down a San Diego freeway like a bat out of hell, or like a woman approaching middle age who couldn't carry any more hurt in her body, keep in mind that it was the non-slit-your-throat choice, even if it wasn't very far away from that choice.

Boom.

Head-on collision.

Boom.

Jail.

Boom.

DUI.

I think we can all agree, huge failure, right?

And yet.

I was arrested. I went to jail. I was let out and given community service as well as mandatory drug and alcohol group counseling.

What's important to pause and think about here is that had I been a person of color, my fate would have been far worse. This is why I say that my story isn't the most important one to listen to. My hope is that by contributing a tiny piece of my story to the larger world of stories, I can help us hear and see all the stories differently. We are nothing without each other, and it's time we admit that we are actually pieces of each other.

Here are some of the pieces of the story that followed. Because I totaled my car, I was carless and without a valid license for a year. A graduate student in my MFA fiction writing class offered to let me borrow one of his cars. Maybe he felt sorry for me, or maybe he felt compassion, or maybe he thought I was pathetic, or maybe he was trying to save me. I'll have to ask him what role he thinks he played in that story. He drove me to my mandatory community service jobs. He drove me and picked me up from my mandatory group counseling sessions. He drove me and picked me up from my mandatory AA meetings. What he didn't do, ever, was judge me. No one in my life ever did that before. Resisted judging me. We began spending time together.

I was fired for having sex with that student. He was twenty-nine. It felt like I was fired for falling in love outside the lines.

Fired, as in failure again. Right?

And yet.

The only happiness I have ever known in my entire puny life is inside the house I live in right now, in Portland, Oregon. The man that cost me my job? The one I married from that strange swirl of chaotic events? He is the love of my life. For more than seventeen years now. And the joy that came from our tangling narratives, my son, who is now sixteen, is nothing short of a sort of secular version of heaven, to me, given what happened with my daughter, given the unfortunate family I started out with.

In other words, the portals of failure opened up into my entire life.

And I'm not alone.

● ● ●

I met my friend Jason Arias when he showed up in a fiction writing class at the community college where I teach. He was quiet, tall, sat in the back, very observant. The first story he turned in had the skill and wit and depth of Raymond Carver. I'm not kidding you. His story blew my face off. I thought, *What the hell is* this *guy doing in my class?* But as the class continued, I soon understood what he was doing there. He was doing the same thing I did when I got spit out of the regular flow of things, when I flunked out of college and got into too much trouble . . . he was trying to claw his way back into the socius. One story at a time. This is Jason's story:

The word misfit *makes me think of the punk band the Misfits. It makes me think of how the lyrics to their song "We Are 138"*

have been theoretically tied to everything—from Nazi Germany
(Hermann Göring's IQ), to the first George Lucas film (THX 1138),
to the Federal Reserve (using numerology)—and that somebody
should just fucking ask [Glenn] Danzig what those lyrics actually
mean already. The Nazi Germany theory of the song makes me
think of Viktor Frankl (a neurologist, Holocaust survivor turned
author) who published the book Man's Search for Meaning. *How*
Frankl outlived friends and neighbors and family, and by the end
of the book states that life is meaningless; that it's each person's
responsibility to give it meaning. That life's just a blank canvas, an
untagged wall. That until we fill that shit up with color—or play
further with the concepts of black and white contrast, or rock sepia
in hip swaying, heartfelt ways—life will continue to be meaningless.

But all Frankl pointed out was a truth that on some level we al-
ready know. It's a survival mechanism to identify with something,
to believe in something. We take on a concept and embody it. And
sometimes these identities consume us. I've loved people that have
and/or do self-identify as firefighters, authors, artists, soldiers,
punks, drug dealers, addicts, gangsters, bed wetters, survivors,
victims, mothers, fathers, librarians, and others.

Personally, I have identified as a bastard, a son, a brother, a pro-
tector, a failure, a rocker, a sinner, off-white, a wannabe, partially
black, a father, semi-brown, a husband, a firefighter, mulatto,
a thinker, an "other," an idiot, a victor, a pretender, a writer, a
striver. But it's always changing, the idea of what I am, of what I
should be, is always disproving itself. And I wonder if that is what
a misfit is—somebody who tries on every pantsuit and street-wear
montage only to crudely tailor them up? So we wear these patchwork

quilts, or go naked, but we're always searching, always striving.

Growing up we moved a lot; changed schools some. Mom had a run of bad boyfriends. Humor was a kind of magical buffer. It made Mom laugh. It made my peers smile. My family didn't have much money, but I liked that. I felt like it made us (my sister, my mom, and me) stronger, tighter. I think I was able to insulate in this way, to live in my own mythology. There was the world and then there was our world. Maybe it was the world against us, but not in any angst-ridden way. Not yet. Not until I started realizing that my reality wasn't reality.

I think my real problems with authority began at age twelve. Me, being choked with both hands by a downtown cop because my friend threw his nacho container off a bridge beneath which the Portland Rose Festival passed. Me, a straight-A student at the time but not looking it. Looking like a mulatto kid wearing a Metallica T-shirt and a dangling, broadsword earring. The cop thinking the nacho cheese was egg yolk. My friend crying at my side, begging the cop to stop, saying it wasn't eggs. Saying that he thinks I can't breathe. Saying that he's sorry he threw the cheese. My hands on the cop's forearms, pushing them away. My vision blurring. My windpipe constricting. Me, not realizing that that cop's hands would stay wrapped around my neck long after getting released from the Front Avenue precinct. Not charged with anything. Me, not crediting the cop with enough grip strength to last twenty-six years.

After that choking I listened to music louder, grew my hair longer, but kept my grades up. I still gave a shit. That is, until my seventh-grade English teacher—the guy I wanted to be, who'd published books (but told us, his students, that we'd "have to wait until we were older to read them")—slashed his wrists and neck and threw himself off a *bridge over the Willamette River. And I probably would have been able to mourn that teacher, to process it in some semi-healthy way, had he not killed himself because he was being investigated for pedophilia and child pornography. It took me this long (being a grown-ass man) to realize how much that incident fucked with my head. How do you mourn your hero that turns out to be a villain?*

Everything I thought I knew about the world collapsed. My grades started to plummet. I got kicked out of school a couple of months after the suicide. I lasted one month in eighth grade before being expelled again. Somehow they pushed me on to ninth grade with only a two-month stint at another school. My first year of high school was my last year of high school. I traded in my Metallica T-shirts for flannels and bandanas. I worked during the day and raged with my disillusioned clan of mismatched misfits all night. That was my teen years.

A couple of years ago my sister ran into this guy we used to call Indian Johnny and he said, "Your brother's still alive?"

Now I have two sons. I have a respectable job. Most of my "clan" from back then is dead, or serving time, or in and out of rehab. I have a couple friends that made good.

My younger son is a high school junior this year. My older son has already graduated. I don't talk about my teen years with them. I tell them that the world is theirs, if they're ready to work hard enough for what they want. I tell them to imagine their happiest version of life and then work toward it. I tell them that nobody gets anywhere without first graduating high school, and then figuring out college or a trade to invest in. I tell them to make the best choices while they're young.

Yeah, I'm a hypocrite. But only because I love my boys so much more than I used to love myself.

There are two definitions that Merriam-Webster gives for misfit:

1. *something that fits badly*

2. *a person who is poorly adapted to a situation or environment <social misfits>*

I've spent a good portion of my life finding ways of making up for being awkward or poorly adapted to different environments. I've found ways to adapt, blend in, camouflage up. Laughter goes a long way. Compliments go a long way. And some things are just going to be awkward. Sometimes I'm just not going to fit in, and I'm okay with that.

At this point I'm more interested in that first definition of misfit— *how things fit badly. How we store and distort experiences in our bodies. How I lived, worked, and loved with an invisible necklace of cop hands around my neck for years and didn't even know it. That I didn't realize that's what that tightness was in my throat. How I first had to acknowledge that cop hands necklace before addressing it. And the only way I finally got rid of that fucking thing was by giving in to the overwhelming feeling of impending death, and somehow not dying.*

Have you ever been bungee jumping? My wife bought me two jumps for my twenty-first birthday. There was this moment before that first jump when my legs wouldn't respond to my brain's commands. I just stood there, looking down at the river flowing hundreds of feet below me. I had to fight every survival instinct in my body to go over the edge of that bridge. This particular bridge was surrounded by a beautiful Washington State forest. The river was sparkling in the sunlight. The sky was blue with picturesque cumulus clouds mixed in. The only way I took that leap was by telling myself that if something went wrong it would be a beautiful setting to die in, a good day to die. I had to fully give in to the possibility of death. Getting rid of the necklace of invisible cop hands around my neck felt the same way as jumping off that bridge. It felt terrifying, and increasingly dangerous, and unbelievably freeing. And maybe that's what a misfit is to me: someone with the ability to become increasingly dangerous, in incredibly loving ways, and not care what people think about it. I don't know if I fall into that category.

All right, I'm feeling naked again.

The Misfits' former guitarist Bobby Steele had an interesting story behind the meaning of the song "We Are 138." He called it "Glenn [Danzig]'s biggest joke on his fans." Steele said that Danzig told him it was from a character in the book I, Robot. But according to Steele, there's no character with that name. Steele also said that Danzig once told him, "If someone asks what it means, we should just laugh, and in a mocking tone say 'What? You don't know?'"

I think a misfit knows when they meet another misfit, even if they're both all camouflaged up. We emit a pheromone or something. Maybe we share similarities in our hidden pasts. I don't know.

But hey, Lidia, ask me the question "Do you identify with the word misfit?" again.

I think I've got a better answer for it. Misfits can turn a story on a dime. Eye wink. Head nod. Forehead sweat. Side smile.

•   •   •

It's true, I too can spot a fellow misfit a mile away. Jason Arias shares a bloodline with me. Or if not a bloodline, then a heart line, a story line. News flash! I might fuck up again. As a matter of fact, I'm quite certain I will. But it will not mean I'm nothing. It will never mean I'm nothing again. My mistakes will live on in me, when I'm doing well, and when I'm diving back down into the depths again. They are as much a part of me as any success or good thing I ever do.

So what's the matter with me? With Jason? With Sean, Mary, Jordan and Domi, with Zach, Melissa, Althea and Melanie? With misfits?

When I look up at the night sky, I no longer imagine things like heaven or hell or a godhead. I see all of matter and energy. I see my father, who was our abuser, but who also introduced me to art, architecture, film, and novels. I see my mother, who failed to save her daughters, but who also gave us strong and independent imaginations, so strong that we reimagined our stories away from home and into the world. I see my friend Bennett, who ended his life some years after we were in Ken Kesey's writing class together. I see Kesey too, who told me to never surrender. I see Kurt Cobain and Virginia Woolf and Freddie Mercury and Marguerite Duras and David Bowie and Prince and Philip Seymour Hoffman and Mary Shelley—personal totems to me.

I see my mother, Dorothy, and my daughter, Lily.

I see everything we are or were as stars stitched so beautifully across the night sky, it takes your breath away.

If misfits have a song, let our song be the night sky. Where even dead light shines.

Love Letter to Fellow Misfits

I'm just like you. I'm moving through my life one day at a time, and sometimes, on the hard days, even an hour at a time. I'm trying to help us remember that we invent our own beauty and our own paths and our own bent, weird ways of doing things, and that they're not nothing and they matter, too. We're the half of culture that doesn't take the paths that are lying right in front of us. Our song may be a little off-key, but it's a kind of beauty, too. I know I'm not the only person who thought that up, but I can sure stand up and help remind us not to give up, that we have a song, too.

Wherever you are, you are not alone, even in your aloneness. I can hear you. And I am smiling.

ACKNOWLEDGMENTS

Oceans of thanks to Michelle Quint for her patient editorial help as I wove my way through narratives of misfittery.

Thank you beyond forever to Helen Walters at TED, and to my beloved agent, Rayhané Sanders.

All love and gratitude to Sean Davis, Mary Thompson, Melanie Alldritt, Domi Shoemaker, Jordan Foster, Althea Heusties-Wolf, Jason Arias, Melissa Febos, and Zach Ellis, fellow misfits, heart and art warriors.

Introduction

1   www.urbandictionary.com

Chapter 1

2   www.goodreads.com

Chapter 5

3   http://www.newyorker.com/culture/
cultural-comment/praise-rudolph

ABOUT THE AUTHOR

Lidia Yuknavitch is the author of the national bestselling novels *The Book of Joan* and *The Small Backs of Children*, winner of the 2016 Oregon Book Award's Ken Kesey Award for Fiction, as well as the Reader's Choice Award; the novel *Dora: A Headcase*; and the acclaimed memoir *The Chronology of Water*, which was a finalist for a PEN Center USA award for creative nonfiction and winner of a PNBA Award and the Readers' Choice Oregon Book Award. She founded the workshop series Corporeal Writing in Portland, Oregon, where she also teaches Women's Studies, Film Studies, Writing, and Literature. She received her doctorate in literature from the University of Oregon. Her acclaimed TED Talk, "The Beauty of Being a Misfit," has nearly two million views. She lives in Oregon with her husband, Andy Mingo, and their renaissance-man son, Miles. She is a very good swimmer.

WATCH LIDIA YUKNAVITCH'S TED TALK

Lidia Yuknavitch's TED Talk, available for free at TED.com, is the companion to *The Misfit's Manifesto*.

PHOTO: BRET HARTMAN

Andrew Solomon
How the worst moments in our lives make us who we are
Writer Andrew Solomon has spent his career telling stories of the hardships of others. Now he turns inward, bringing us into a childhood of adversity, while also spinning tales of the courageous people he's met in the years since. In a moving, heartfelt, and at times downright funny talk, Solomon gives a powerful call to action to forge meaning from our biggest struggles.

Chimamanda Ngozi Adichie
The danger of a single story
Our lives, our cultures, are composed of many overlapping stories. Novelist Chimamanda Adichie tells the story of how she found her authentic cultural voice—and warns that if we hear only a single story about another person or country, we risk a critical misunderstanding.

Karen Thompson
What fear can teach us
Imagine you're a shipwrecked sailor. You can choose one of three directions and save yourself and your shipmates—but each choice comes with a fearful consequence too. How do you choose? In telling the story of the whaleship *Essex*, novelist Karen Thompson Walker shows how fear propels imagination.

Alyssa Monks
How loss helped one artist find beauty in imperfection
Painter Alyssa Monks finds beauty and inspiration in the unknown, the unpredictable and even the awful. In a poetic, intimate talk, she describes the interaction of life, paint, and canvas through her development as an artist, and as a human.

Who Are You, Really?
The Surprising Puzzle of Personality
by Brian Little

Chances are you probably have a pretty fixed idea of what makes you, you. But what if your personality was flexible, and ultimately in your control? Acclaimed psychologist Brian Little reveals that personality is far more malleable than we imagine.

Why Dinosaurs Matter
by Kenneth Lacovara

Join world-renowned paleontologist Dr. Kenneth Lacovara on a remarkable journey—back to when dinosaurs roamed the Earth—to discover fundamental truths about our own humanity. An urgent reminder that our place on this planet is precarious and potentially fleeting, and that we must look to the past to protect our future.

When Strangers Meet
How People You Don't Know Can Transform You
by Kio Stark

When Strangers Meet reveals the transformative possibility of talking to people you don't know—how these beautiful interruptions in daily life can change you and the world we share. Kio Stark argues for the surprising pleasures of talking to strangers.

Asteroid Hunters
by Carrie Nugent

Everyone's got questions about asteroids. What are they and where do they come from? And most urgently: Are they going to hit earth? Asteroid hunter Carrie Nugent reveals everything we know about asteroids, and how new technology may help us prevent a natural disaster.

ABOUT TED BOOKS

TED Books are small books about big ideas. They're short enough to read in a single sitting, but long enough to delve deep into a topic. The wide-ranging series covers everything from architecture to business, space travel to love, and is perfect for anyone with a curious mind and an expansive love of learning.

Each TED Book is paired with a related TED Talk, available online at TED.com. The books pick up where the talks leave off. An 18-minute speech can plant a seed or spark the imagination, but many talks create a need to go deeper, to learn more, to tell a longer story. TED Books fill this need.

TED is a nonprofit devoted to spreading ideas, usually in the form of short, powerful talks (eighteen minutes or less) but also through books, animation, radio programs, and events. TED began in 1984 as a conference where Technology, Entertainment, and Design converged, and today covers almost every topic— from science to business to global issues—in more than 100 languages. Meanwhile, independently run TEDx events help share ideas in communities around the world.

TED is a global community, welcoming people from every discipline and culture who seek a deeper understanding of the world. We believe passionately in the power of ideas to change attitudes, lives, and, ultimately, our future. On TED.com, we're building a clearinghouse of free knowledge from the world's most inspired thinkers—and a community of curious souls to engage with ideas and each other, both online and at TED and TEDx events around the world, all year long.

In fact, everything we do—from the TED Radio Hour to the projects sparked by the TED Prize, from the global TEDx community to the TED-Ed lesson series — is driven by this goal: How can we best spread great ideas?

TED is owned by a nonprofit, nonpartisan foundation.